The WISDOM of the BODY

"*The Wisdom of the Body* met me where I was and transported me to a place I haven't been in a long time, drawing me across sacred thresholds and inviting me to pause, breathe, and renew my commitment to live life with attention and intention. Thank you, Christine Valters Paintner, for the gift of this book, this vision, this invitation!"

Mary DeTurris Poust
Catholic blogger and author of *Cravings*

"Christine Valters Paintner is a trusted guide, lighting the way home to body and soul. Sharing from experience with her compassionate voice, she speaks to us personally and offers creative resources, supportive allies, and wisdom from the great spiritual traditions. This book is a good map for the journey to wholeness. I put it at the top of my list to recommend to teachers and students seeking to embody the joy of spiritual life."

Cynthia Winton-Henry
Cofounder of InterPlay

"Christine Valters Paintner is a stunningly gifted teacher; I am so grateful that she shares her wisdom on women and embodiment in this latest book. Christine's ability to weave multifaceted spiritual practice with the expressive arts in a sensitive and trauma-informed manner has long inspired me, and I know that many will be helped and inspired through this work. Christine is a true gem, a blessing, and a beacon of light to those of us who are on the path of healing—she is gentle, wise, and challenging in a harmonious blend that comes through in her spirit-filled teachings."

Jamie Marich
Clinical trauma expert and author of *Dancing Mindfulness*

"Christine Valters Paintner has found gems from the Christian tradition—from scripture, the saints, and the Desert Fathers and Mothers—and combined them with other practices such as dance, yoga, and poetry to create an eclectic, hands-on book sure to deepen your spirituality. A mini-retreat you can take at your own pace, *The Wisdom of the Body* is inspiring and possibly life-changing for those who struggle with body issues but also meaningful for those comfortable within their body."

Heidi Schlumpf
National Catholic Reporter columnist

"Christine Valters Paintner is so much more than a truly fine writer; she's a teacher, a guide, and a friend along the way. In *The Wisdom of the Body*, she once again plumbs ancient monastic wisdom to help solve a contemporary problem: the sad rift between body and soul that too often limits our experience of God."

Paula Huston
Author of *One Ordinary Sunday*

WISDOM of the BODY

A CONTEMPLATIVE JOURNEY TO WHOLENESS FOR WOMEN

CHRISTINE VALTERS PAINTNER

SORIN BOOKS   Notre Dame, Indiana

Unless otherwise indicated, scripture quotations are from *New Revised Standard Version Bible*, copyright © 1989 National Council of the Churches of Christ in the United States of America. Used by permission. All rights reserved.

"Earth Your Dancing Place" © May Swenson. From *May Swenson: Collected Poems* (New York: Library of America, 2013). Used with permission of The Literary Estate of May Swenson. All rights reserved.

"Blessing of the Tears" © Jan L. Richardson. From *In Wisdom's Path: Discovering the Sacred in Every Season* (Orlando: Wanton Gospeller Press, 2012), 68–69. Used with permission. All rights reserved.

Illustrations © 2017 by Karen Newe

---

www.sorinbooks.com

Paperback: ISBN-13 978-1-933495-82-8

E-book: ISBN-13 978-1-933495-83-5

Cover image © iStockphoto.com.

Cover and text design by Brian C. Conley.

Printed and bound in the United States of America.

Library of Congress Cataloging-in-Publication Data is available.

Contents

Introduction

You've been walking in circles, searching. Don't drink
by the water's edge. Throw yourself in. Become the
water. Only then will your thirst end.

—Jeanette Berson

For so long, we have been exiles from our bodies—our holy bodies, our beautiful bodies, our bodies created lovingly by God and sustained and nourished by the earth.

You are beginning the long and beautiful journey home.

In our rush through life, we neglect the body's wisdom. We work through fatigue and illness, pushing our bodies and feeling frustrated when they don't keep up. We look at our physical selves with disdain when parts don't measure up to some external standard, one that is always designed to sell us something.

God became flesh. Christ's Incarnation points to embodiment as one of the most important spiritual journeys we make, and its effect is felt in multiple relationships:

- time (Do we rush through our lives or savor slowness?);
- consumerism (Do we buy into the constant quest for self-improvement or rest into the beauty and bounty of our bodies?);
- food (Do we eat just to fill our hunger, to fill an emptiness, or to truly nourish ourselves?);
- the earth (Do we see ourselves as separate from the earth or in intimate communion?); and

- health care (Do we seek the quick fix or cure and lose patience with the slow process of healing?).

The Christian tradition has left an unfortunate legacy of body denial. And yet the very contemplative practices that are so nourishing for our souls can also be directed toward our bodies as a way of plunging into and celebrating the depths of our embodied beings. If we believe that God became flesh, how might we take the incarnation seriously by entering into intimacy with our own bodies?

The word *sin*, when connected with the body, is often used to describe sexual acts. While this isn't a book of sexual ethics, I felt it warranted to mention a definition of sin as alienation from the divine source. How is your body or your feelings about your body alienated from God? You may be carrying a legacy of body shame because of harmful messages from church, family, and culture. Most of us carry some form of this in our history, inhibiting our ability to discover our bodies as sources of love and connection to wisdom. This book helps us overcome that experience of alienation and exile in order to make the beautiful journey home again. In this context we can then discern what feels life-giving for our bodies.

In his book *Touching Enlightenment*, Buddhist author Reginald Ray says the body is the "last unexplored wilderness." He believes that many meditation practices keep us firmly anchored in our heads. The ancient Desert Mothers and Fathers journeyed out to the wilderness of the desert to find God there, at the edges of life, in the places where they felt uncomfortable and God was allowed to be as expansive as possible. In my longing to grow more intimate with the gift of my body, I feel a deeper kinship with those ancient monks called out to the wild edges to discover new ways of being with God. As Ray suggests, our bodies are a wondrous wilderness just waiting for our attention.

This book is an invitation into the wilderness. In these pages, you will be invited to learn ways to stay with yourself in this new and sometimes frightening place until the vastness of the holy is unearthed right within you. The wilderness calls us to be with life's messiness, to relinquish our desire to control what is happening, and to enter wholeheartedly into life's unfolding. To help you embrace the wilderness, you will be invited to integrate contemplative practices and develop new ways of being in relationship with your body, a body that is renewing, is wise, and offers you endless depth, as well as renewed trust.

This book is rooted in the conviction that our bodies offer us the deepest wisdom—wisdom that can guide us through the river of life. The more we deepen into the body's wisdom, the more we will find greater freedom, joy, nourishment, rest, and empowerment for exquisite self-care. This is the contemplative practice. This is the journey into the "last unexplored wilderness."

Introduction to Expressive Arts

Throughout this material you will be invited into different forms of creative expression. The expressive arts will offer us a language and way of expressing our new discoveries and having them witnessed. We can tell our stories in symbolic language, giving them shape, form, and new perspective.

We practice art-making as a journey of exploration, discovery, and prayer. Our aim in art-making isn't to create a beautiful product and impress others but to pay attention to the process of unfolding that leads to the creation of something that authentically expresses our experience in the moment. We welcome in the discomfort and resistance as well as the ease and joy. When we create what is truly within us rather than what we want others to see, we dance on the wild edges and expand our understanding of the Spirit's movement in our lives.

Art can be a journey of revelation and truth telling. Creating from the heart—as opposed to the mind or ego—draws us closer to the Great Artist who is continuously at work in the world and with whom we can collaborate on life's artistry. Art also helps us to connect to the body's wisdom because it drops us out of our logical analysis and desire to control and into an intuitive awareness that arises from the body.

The expressive arts developed as a way to integrate the various art forms and to honor each one as a unique language of the soul. Working with the arts in an interdisciplinary and connected way offers deeper insight than when used in isolation from each other.

Central to the expressive arts is an emphasis on process. We are not concerned with product, with what something will look like. We enter the art-making experience as a journey of discovery. We stay present to what comes up along the way. We notice the moments in which judgment arises, and we breathe, stay present, and gently let judgment go.

As you create, notice when you want to control the process. That is your rational, thinking mind entering in. Notice when you get lost in time and space. Notice when you are fully in the unknown and not anxious about that as you simply attend to what unfolds before you in creation. That is your body's wisdom holding the space.

Introduction to Yin Yoga and Conscious Dance

I first discovered yoga as a child. My aunt taught me some of the poses, and I loved the way my body felt as I moved into them. I was never an athletic person, but I was naturally flexible, so it was a gift to have a physical practice that felt good in my body. Years later, in my twenties, I was reintroduced to yoga while I was on disability from work. I was gifted to find a gentle teacher who showed me ways that yoga could help me be present with my body in kindness and compassion as it went through the slow process of healing.

When I lived in Seattle, Washington, I discovered an amazing yoga studio called Samarya Center. Their website displayed a diversity of body images, and I could see people who looked like me in those photos. My experience of practicing there was a sense of coming home. They also wove principles of yoga philosophy into the classes, and I found that the wisdom of those ancient texts had much kinship with the stories I love so much from the Desert Mothers and Fathers. I eventually completed their two-hundred-hour yoga teacher training because of my own desire to move more deeply into my yoga practice, and I discovered that I loved to offer this contemplative practice to others as well.

Some of you may already have a yoga practice, and for some it may be an uncomfortable idea or one that has never appealed to you. Part of my personal meditation practice includes yin yoga, which is a way of practicing yoga where poses are held for generally three to five minutes. On a physical level the long hold times stretch the fascia, which is the layer of connective tissue beneath your muscles. On a spiritual level, the invitation to sit with discomfort and wait is a profound practice. I find those minutes are a time when I can really explore what is happening within my body and bring my breath to places of tightness. It is a time of honoring and listening.

If you want to try the yoga practices suggested here, I would strongly recommend investing in a good yoga mat, a block, and a bolster. Yin yoga benefits from extra support for different poses to really help our muscles relax while holding for extended periods of time. If any pose suggested doesn't work for your body, you can try simply imagining your body in the pose, knowing that this energetic connection gives us many of the same benefits.

My rediscovery of my love of dance happened more recently at a BodySoul Rhythms retreat in Santa Fe, New Mexico, several years ago. This is a Jungian-based creative practice that engages the body to explore dreams and fairy tales. It was in that space that I uncovered some of the layers that hid my inner dancer from myself. In that step toward freedom I began exploring many conscious dance practices such as 5Rhythms, SoulMotion, Open Floor, and InterPlay.

Conscious dance is essentially dance as a practice of meditation and awareness, and it has no steps. The idea is to tune into how the body wants to move and let the dance unfold from there. It is movement that is inner directed and improvisational, beginning with the dancer's attention on the body and how it wants to move in any given moment. Impulses arise offering wisdom and insight, generating a direction for movement or stillness. The conscious, thinking mind lets go of control and direction and observes while impulses are allowed to take form.

The body speaks truth if we would only learn how to listen. When we drop down out of the spinning voices of the mind, telling its tales of anxiety and calling us back into the past or out into the future, the body calls us full present here and now. This, right now, is the only moment for the body. Physical practices help us to anchor our awareness in our bodies rather than our minds.

We find freedom in these body practices and in the dance in which they call us to participate. We begin to discern new paths that are body guided. We start to live in rhythms and cycles that are nourishing rather than depleting. We touch a primal joy that is our birthright.

It's possible that the whole idea of somehow acknowledging your body as an aspect of your spirituality, let alone your wholeness, feels not only foreign but also frightening. You don't know if you'll be able to do it. You're not a yoga or dance person. You only think about your breath when you're winded. *You are welcome here.* Everything you are feeling is welcome, too. The pages ahead will be a beautiful introduction into a sacredness you've not yet explored but that waits for you with open and embodied arms.

Movement as Medicine

When you dance I recommend creating a sacred space. This might mean an altar (chapter 3 has some suggestions for how to create an altar). Even just lighting a candle can signal your intention to make this practice a prayer rather than merely "exercise." When your intention is to enter into the wisdom of your body, and to allow your body as much as possible unimpeded movement as an expression of unnamed desires, it is a prayer and a holy act.

Movement becomes a sacred medicine that heals the disconnection so many of us experience day after day from our beautiful bodies. It is a medicine that helps us to address the places we feel blocked or afraid and allows us to honor those experiences and dance beyond their confinement. As we dance we discover places of rigidity and holding, stiffness and pain. We can respond with gentleness and opening.

If you are in too much pain to dance, try dancing in your imagination. Find a quiet place to lie down, put on a piece of music, and then imagine yourself dancing. There is a physical effect. Or you can try just dancing with one hand, a practice that is introduced in chapter 1.

When you feel stuck as to how to move, try just shaking your body. Animals shake to reorganize and calm their nervous systems and to shake off stressful experiences. Begin by shaking one hand as vigorously as you can and then the other. Then shake one leg while bracing against a wall. Then shake the other leg. Then shake out what you sit on. Shake out your voice by vocalizing some sounds. You might imagine as you are shaking that you are setting free whatever you don't need to hold on to.

Before You Get Started

Here are some considerations as you begin this work:

1. *Dressing for movement*: For the movement practices, wear comfortable, nonrestrictive clothing. Whatever feels good to move in is a perfect choice. Avoid clothing that is too long or might inhibit your movement. When dancing on a noncarpeted floor such as wood or tile, either going barefoot or wearing shoes that support your feet is a safer choice than wearing socks.

2. *Contemplative presence*: This practice is simply about showing up to your body's experience and noticing sensations, feelings, thoughts, and whatever is happening within you. Continue to draw your awareness back to this moment in time, and notice when your awareness is drawn elsewhere. When you find your thoughts drifting, instead of judging yourself, simply bring your awareness back with compassion and care.

3. *Honor your body's limits*: At any time if you feel pain, stop immediately. Listen to your body's needs in a given practice, and never push past the place where your body can safely go. This work is not about performance but about tuning into your body's needs and responding with love.

4. *Return to stillness*: At any time during your movement practice feel free to take a break for reflection, quietness, or even a drink of water. Stillness is as essential to your body awareness as is movement; they work together.

5. *Emotional safety*: Sometimes movement can bring up distressing experiences in our bodies. Have someone you can call if needed during

these times—a trusted friend, a spiritual director, or a counselor. Honor the needs of your heart as well.

Overview of Chapters

We will explore a variety of practices drawn primarily from desert, Celtic, and Benedictine monastic traditions as well as body-based practices from yin yoga and dance. These will become our holy well offering generous drink. As we drop down beneath the chattering of our thoughts and the endless stories they tell, we discover a place of stillness and wisdom, a source of deep joy and praise.

In chapter 1 we are introduced to St. Hildegard of Bingen, a twelfth-century Benedictine abbess who developed the concept of *viriditas*, or the greening power of God, which can become an important discernment principle for us as we seek to nourish ourselves. Chapter 2 introduces the breath as the first gateway into an experience of the body and is rooted in the ancient desert monks and their practice of breath prayer. In chapter 3 we explore the senses as another portal into experiencing our bodies' knowledge, and we learn to savor and celebrate the delights the senses offer to us. Chapter 4 invites us into an exploration of our feelings and how to practice hospitality to our emotional landscape. Chapter 5 turns our attention to thoughts, which so often are the source of our self-criticism and judgment, and we glean wisdom from the desert monks in working with them.

Chapter 6 invites us into an exploration of our experience of exile from our bodies and the grief that arises, calling us to a powerful act of lament. We dive more explicitly into the Incarnation in chapter 7 and focus on the way God becoming flesh calls us back to our bodies as sources of deep wisdom and grace. Chapter 8 introduces the idea of ecstasy, found in the writings of many of the Christian mystics, as a call back to the joy that is our birthright. Chapter 9 invites us to consider the intimate connection between our own physical bodies and the earth body. Chapter 10 brings everything we have explored together into a final consideration of our bodies as intimately tied to our vocations and the journey back home.

This material was offered in the format of an online retreat in 2014 and 2015. I am deeply grateful to the women who participated and helped to refine this work. With their permission I include some of their poetic reflections in response to the materials and exercises just to offer windows of possibility.

How to Work with This Book

> Be strong then, and enter into your own body; there you
> have a solid place for your feet.
>
> —Kabir

This is not a book about Christian ethics or morality but an invitation into experience. My invitation to you is to an encounter with your own holy embodied self. I will offer you a variety of reflections, practices, meditations, and experiences that can open you to an encounter with the sacredness of your physical being.

You will be invited into body practices including yoga and dance or movement. If these feel like unfamiliar territory, you are most welcome to step in gently, even tentatively. Go at your own pace, and see what stirs your delight and curiosity.

As with most of the books I write, this one is meant as more of a journey and process than a quick read. I highly recommend you work through each chapter slowly over the course of a week or a month, in tegrating the ideas and practices and engaging in the art explorations. If you find yourself wanting to rush and get through the chapter, notice that without judgment. Reflect on your own tendencies to rush what you're experiencing, and ask what it is trying to reveal to you. Perhaps there is discomfort arising or impatience with the long, slow journey of this work. This is all a process, and we can honor the fact that even these things we call resistance can be used to inform our journey.

The invitation is to a deep transformation of your relationship to your body, a relationship that takes time to renew. Even better than accepting this invitation alone is if you can join a partner, a soul friend, or a small group and gather regularly to work through each chapter and discuss what insights arise together.

Body Journal

I recommend making a body journal. Find a blank book where you can work through this material and mark the thresholds on the journey. Include your poems, reflections, and other art here. Write down your responses to the invitations and to your movement experiences. Let this be a place of profound self-honesty and compassion, a place where you can begin again and again without judgment, simply embracing the joy of always coming back to the road home. Consider decorating the cover with images that make you feel alive. Be conscious of unhealthy body images presented to us in magazine advertisements that we sometimes strive to emulate. Let this be a place to encourage a celebration of your wholeness rather than a sense of what you are lacking.

Seeking Support

If you are struggling with an eating disorder, I encourage you to find support from a qualified therapist or counselor through the National Eating Disorders Association. This book offers a variety of spiritual practices to connect more deeply with your body, but it's not a replacement for medical support when needed.

There may be some of you suffering from trauma in your bodies. Nothing here should substitute for medical advice, and I recommend finding a trusted and trained counselor who can accompany you as you move through these chapters.

I recommend that anyone moving into this material with a sincere heart and commitment find a soul friend with whom to confide and perhaps share the journey.

Blessings As We Begin

> We carry a terrible wound: alienation
>   from our embodied life.
> Your flesh shall become a great poem.
>
> —Walt Whitman

Welcome to this journey. I want to keep saying that again and again. Welcome and more welcome. Know yourself—*all* of yourself: all your doubts and resistance, your body and soul, and your joy and your grief—as welcome. My deepest hope for this time is that, after journeying through all ten chapters, you might discover yourself welcoming in even more of your beautiful being and your places of resistance might begin to soften.

Two of the things I like to teach over and over are this kind of radical hospitality, which takes a lifetime of practice, and gentleness with yourself—probably because I need both of these so much myself.

Our bodies have this unfortunate tendency to carry with them a lifetime of criticism, analysis, scrupulous dissection, anger, betrayal, and more. Removing that burden requires that we begin to remember ourselves as created out of God's great love. When one of my teaching partners, Betsey Beckman, offers up her story dance of the creation story from Genesis, she embodies God as Creator, and with each act of creation she says, "That's *good*," with unbridled enthusiasm—not in a distanced and unaffected way but in a delighted and deeply celebratory way. Can we remember this? Can we imagine the Divine uttering those words over every nook of our own creation?

The root of the word *remember* means to make whole again, to bring the parts back together. We have been waging a war on ourselves for too long, tearing ourselves apart. As Walt Whitman writes, this alienation from our embodied life is a great wound we each carry.

What might it mean for you to allow your flesh to become a great poem?

Chapter 1

Viriditas:
Claiming New Body Stories

This is your body, your greatest gift, pregnant with wisdom you do not hear, grief you thought was forgotten, and joy you have never known.

—Marion Woodman, *Coming Home to Myself*

Like many of you reading, I have spent much of my lifetime struggling with my body in a variety of ways. I remember using food to fill the pain of addicted parents from as early as the age of eight; I used it even more when my mother died suddenly in my early thirties. I was diagnosed with a serious autoimmune illness at the age of twenty-one, the same one that had devastated my mother's body, and I spent a year in my midtwenties on disability. I have carried self-loathing and self-consciousness, ambivalence, and a sense of betrayal for too many years.

I share these things because I want you to know that this pilgrimage into the sometimes beautiful and often terrifying world of our bodies is a journey and a process. I want you to know that I walk alongside you in seeking a deeper, more compassionate, and wiser relationship to the tremendous grace that is my body. I want you to know that the person guiding you in this process has really wrestled with many of the same things you have.

I still wrestle at times. But I have also found, through the contemplative path, an enormous gift in my body, even when I don't feel great. I have come to love and cherish my body's wisdom in its many dimensions, and I continue to practice listening, learning, and loving. I have come to such tenderness and appreciation for the ways my body is companion and guide. I have also had experiences of profound beauty and grace in my body while holding a pose in yoga and feeling my strength and flexibility, surrendering to the dance and shedding my self-consciousness, making love to my beloved husband, eating a gorgeous meal with friends, and walking by the edge of the sea and feeling wind and water revitalize me.

Each of you, too, has stories such as these: stories of suffering, stories of delight. I want you to know I am with you. Your story will be different, yet some elements will feel familiar. I encourage you to honor the full spectrum of the story with your body but to also lay aside old stories that keep you mired in old ways of thinking, that limit your freedom and movement. Although grief is welcome and there is a chapter dedicated to welcoming in those feelings, this journey isn't about dwelling in your wounded places. When you notice yourself thinking as you read this book something such as *I don't do that* or *my body doesn't move that way*, be honoring of your limits while also gently challenging the voices that show up to see if they are telling the truth. So often they are not.

We may also encounter ambivalence around the Christian story. For those of us rooted in the Christian tradition, we are likely familiar with all the ways our religion and its traditions teach us mixed messages about our bodies at best and outright disdain for our physical selves at worst. Even if we don't locate ourselves in the Christian tradition, the legacy is there in the culture, voices of shame, and rampant marketing designed to feed our insecurities and sense of dissatisfaction.

And yet this journey is not about telling those old stories, continuing to get stuck in them.

I could spend these pages and many more diving into the deep roots of our body wounding through religion, culture, and family. But my inclination is that a more helpful and transformative place to spend our time is in the invitation into presence and in learning ways to really listen to what our bodies are saying rather than getting stuck in the thoughts and judgments we have about our bodies. We will explore ways to work with thoughts in chapter 5.

Together we are invited to create something new. We are drawing from the deep well of contemplative wisdom and practices to weave together a new vision, one that honors the profundity of incarnation, of God become flesh. The enormity of that claim for our relationship to our physical selves and the material world is profound.

Viriditas as a Discernment Principle

> I am the living breath in a human being placed in a tabernacle of marrow, veins, bones, and flesh, giving it vitality and supporting its every movement.
>
> —St. Hildegard of Bingen, *Scivias* I 4:4

Hildegard of Bingen was a twelfth-century Benedictine abbess known for being a theologian, visionary, musical composer, spiritual director, preacher, and healer. For centuries monasteries have been centers of healing and herbal medicine. Monks would grow the herbs and learn their applications so that people would come for both spiritual and physical healing.

We are losing this connection between spiritual and physical healing as medicine takes place in the efficient and sterile halls of hospitals. Please don't misunderstand me: I am profoundly grateful for the gifts of modern medicine and rely on it to some degree to maintain my own quality of life. Yet we have lost so much in this shift from the model of slow medicine and healing to the pursuit of quick cures. We compartmentalize ourselves, seeking the fix for the headache or the stomach trouble without considering the whole of our bodies and our lives. We become impatient when illness descends rather than yielding to the body's needs and desires.

We rarely have a relationship with our doctors, spending only minutes with them each visit, whereas Hildegard, and other monastics like her, would have known her patients. She would have seen the profound connection between body and soul. She would have practiced slow medicine. She was an immensely practical woman who also saw the life of the body and soul as intimately intertwined. In an age when many distanced themselves from the body's needs, she embraced the body as an essential portal to our experience of the Divine through the gift of our senses.

One of the fundamental principles of Hildegard's worldview is *viriditas*, which means the "greening power of God." Even more than that, it refers to a lushness and fecundity in the world, a greening life force we can witness in forests, gardens, and farmland. Hildegard, who lived in the valley around the river Rhine in Germany, was profoundly impacted by her witness to the profusion of greenness and how this green life energy was a sign of abundance and life. It is what sustains and animates us.

Greenness is not just a physical reality but a spiritual one as well. Hildegard believed that viriditas was something to be cultivated in both body and soul. Her language is filled with metaphors for seeking out the moistness and fruitfulness of the soul. The sign of our aliveness is this participation in the life force of the Creator. Anything that blocks this flow through us contributes to both physical disease and spiritual unrest. For Hildegard, *viriditas* was always experienced in tension with *ariditas*, which is the opposite experience of dryness, barrenness, and shriveling up. She would keep asking how to bring the flow of greening life energy back in fullness to a person.

Victoria Sweet, a medical doctor in San Francisco and researcher in medieval history, wrote a wonderful book called *God's Hotel: A Doctor, a Hospital, and a Pilgrimage to the Heart of Medicine* in which she explored Hildegard's principles of greening in her own medical practice. Dr. Sweet worked in a long-term care facility and began to ask what was blocking a patient's access to this life-giving greening energy; shifting her perspective enabled her to find healing paths that were previously unseen. She also discovered that simply being in relationship with her patients over time allowed her to see patterns and behaviors that revealed far more into their care than a quick visit could ever do. Her experience shows what slow medicine might look like in our increasingly fragmented and rushed world.

Seeking Nourishment

Nothing will ever dazzle you
like the dreams of your body.

—Mary Oliver, "Humpbacks"

This poem is a beautiful place to begin this journey because it offers us a concrete image to hold as we move through the time and questions ahead: How do I welcome all that is most nourishing and fruitful into my body and soul? What are the habits and beliefs that rob me of this fertile moistness in my body and soul?

There is a story from the Desert Fathers where an Abba says to a seeker, "Do not give your heart to that which does not satisfy your heart."[1] This can be easier said than done since we are inclined to so many comforts that only serve to numb and distract us from life. How often do we try to satisfy ourselves with that which depletes us?

In the book of Deuteronomy we hear a similar invitation: "I have set before you life and death, blessings and curses. Choose life so that you and your descendants may live" (Dt 30:19). Choose what is life-giving and what makes you flourish.

What if your fundamental commitment as you begin this journey is to only offer your body and soul that which is nourishing, to listen to what depletes you and say no to those things? I invite you to hold the following question as you move forward: Does this nourish me or does this deplete me?

I find some of the contemporary materials on intuitive eating very inspiring and sound. And yet, for some of us, if we have engaged in disordered eating of any kind, tuning back into that intuition can be challenging. The contemplative path is about deepening our capacity for intuitive connection to our body wisdom so we begin to hear our bodies' voices.

Sometimes we will only discover in retrospect whether something was nourishing or not. Keep returning to those questions of nourishment and depletion and notice what is true for you in this moment, not what was true some time ago or what you long for in the future. The body grounds us here and now.

Is this truly nourishing? If not, can I change what I am doing? If I can't change what I am doing, can I shift my perspective? Can I pay attention to how my body feels in this experience and make room for whatever that might be? Can I offer a prayer on behalf of someone in need? Can I commit to myself that I will do something nourishing when this necessary task is completed?

Our work with this process—and it is a lifetime process—is simply about presence and awareness rather than judgment. Through presence we practice a radical hospitality to our own experience. If I eat too much or spend hours in front of the television mindlessly, can I welcome in my disappointment with myself? Can I welcome in the grief I am trying to avoid feeling?

Accept that there will be times when you do something that doesn't feel especially good for your body or soul. Then go back to my invitation to be ever so gentle with yourself. When we experience resistance and then we refuse to embrace the resistance, we further our own wounding. One of the most healing practices I have found is this simple act of kindness and deep care for our well-being.

The practice is exactly that, a practice. We get to show up again and again.

Bring this question to everything: to eating, to work, to playing, and to movement. Sometimes we are required to perform tasks for work that aren't nourishing, and that is okay. But bringing our awareness to the moment can help to wake us to new possibilities.

Then notice the patterns. So much of what we describe as nourishing are things to be enjoyed slowly and are rooted in the experience of the body: nourishing food, good conversation, time spent in nature, and rest. In contrast, what depletes us are often things such as worry, anxiety, control, conflict, and rushing, many things that reside in our mind and thoughts. Notice what is true for you. How do you define true nourishment?

The body loves slowness. Slowness creates more space for greening to enter our being, allowing us to experience the lushness of the body. Of course, the contemplative loves slowness as well. For me, the heart of the contemplative path is slowing down and paying attention, becoming fully present.

When we get anxious we become disconnected from ourselves; our thoughts start to race and grasp. When we are always running from one thing to another, we lose ourselves and a fundamental connection to the body.

Ally on the Journey: Hildegard of Bingen

> O Eternal God, now may it please you
> to burn in love
> so that we become the limbs
> fashioned in the love you felt
> when you begot your Son
> at the first dawn
> before all creation.
>
> —Hildegard of Bingen, *O eterne deus*

In each chapter I will invite you to call in the presence of a woman mystic or a woman from the scriptures who can act as an ally on this healing journey. These holy women can offer us support and guidance across the ages.

Hildegard of Bingen was an amazing and powerful woman who also struggled greatly with physical ailments throughout her life. She was an herbal healer and wrote a book of plant medicine. People came to her for healing of both body and soul.

Imagine that Hildegard is here with you as you embark on this willing descent into the wilderness of your body. Imagine what she would have to say to you. Imagine you can tell her anything about your body, and listen for what guidance she offers. Ask her to show you the places where your body hungers for more greenness, more nourishment.

What would it be like to move through the day with a sense of having enough—enough love, enough time, enough food, or enough money? So much of our depletion comes from a sense of scarcity, and yet if we just look at the world of herbs, we discover God's generous abundance in plants that heal, offer fragrant delight, and give us pleasure in eating. Can we remember these things as very good? Can we celebrate that there is more than enough? Viriditas reminds us again and again that there is no lack. It is offered to us so freely.

Practice: Stability and Staying with Our Experience

In the Benedictine tradition, monks would take three vows: stability, conversion, and obedience. Stability on one level is a commitment to staying with the same community and monastery for their entire lives. But on another level it is about not running away from things. The call of the monk is to stay in the "cell"—one's own experience—and to stay fully present. The cell for monks was the cave of the heart, that deeply interior place where we encounter the divine spark within us. The inner cell is the place where we show up to do our inner work.

We have so many ways to distract ourselves. Rushing and anxiety make us feel depleted and also pull us right out of our embodied experience. As we make the descent into the wilderness of the body, we will likely find two experiences: a sense of enlivening as we make a deeper connection to our physical selves and start to draw from that wisdom, and a sense of being overwhelmed, grieved, or agitated at beginning to drop down into our embodied experience. We resist our bodies because we are afraid of what we will encounter there. We may find that we want to run very far away.

The vow of stability calls us to stay present, which means staying in this moment: not rushing to the next thing and not allowing anxiety to draw our energy out into worries of the future or to a more comfortable distraction but staying present to what is actually true right in this moment.

The body speaks truth if we would only learn how to listen. When we drop down out of the spinning voices of the mind, telling their tales of anxiety and calling us back into the past or out into the future, the body calls us to be fully present here and now. The only moment for the body is right now.

Perhaps the truth is that I am feeling grief and sadness well up, yet I don't know why. Stability calls us to stay with those emotions, to let them have room to move through us. We don't run away, whether in our thoughts or in our physical being. When we block the flow of our emotional life, we also block the flow of greening in ourselves. Opening on one level creates opening on other levels as well.

When we stay with our experience, we discover that it changes all the time. The grief that felt overwhelming has room for expression and then subsides. As we practice radical hospitality to ourselves in all forms, we begin to draw together those broken pieces and return to wholeness.

Meditation: Greening Power of God

This meditation is a reflection on your experience of the day and can be done either in the evening or the following morning. It is an invitation to pay attention to the patterns of greening and depletion in your life, bringing in an awareness of Hildegard's viriditas through an adapted form of the examen prayer created by Spanish mystic Ignatius of Loyola in the sixteenth century.

Allow yourself five minutes each day to pause and listen for the presence or absence of viriditas in your body and soul. Breathe slowly and deeply. Let yourself soften into this moment. Once you feel yourself resting into the stillness, bring your awareness to your heart center, that place of intuitive knowing. Just notice what you feel, and be with whatever comes up without trying to change it.

Breathe into your heart center, welcoming in this infinite source of compassion. From this perspective of love and grace toward yourself, review the past day in your mind. Ask yourself the following: Where in the last several hours have I experienced the lush greenness and life force in my body and soul? Where did I encounter a sense of vitality, of creativity, of energy, and of being well nourished?

Savor and bring a heart of gratitude for this gift, even if it was the briefest moment. Then shift your awareness, look back on the day again, and ask yourself these questions: In the last several hours, where have I experienced dryness and aridity in my body and soul? Where did I encounter a sense of feeling stretched, overwhelmed, or depleted?

Bring gentleness to yourself and your experience; see if you might offer forgiveness to yourself for any choices you made or to your body for any ways it experienced limitations. Then bring your awareness back to your heart and your breath, and gently return to the room. Allow a few minutes to journal what you noticed. Try this practice over several days and notice any patterns.

Creative Exploration: Mandala Making

Mandalas are circles, which are a universal symbol for wholeness. Many of Hildegard of Bingen's visions appeared to her in mandala form and express the wholeness of the cosmos. All you need is a piece of blank paper and some colored pencils, markers, pens, or crayons. You can do this in your journal. You can use whatever writing implements you have at hand. Notice if you create excuses for yourself about why you can't get to this exploration.

Begin with some centering; this might involve moving into silence, paying attention to your breath, becoming present to your body, and calling your awareness to the sacred presence already with you.

Awaken your energy through gentle movement. Choose a favorite piece of music. Allow a few minutes to let your body move as it longs to, something we rarely do. This is a time to really notice what would feel good and nourishing. Movement will help move your awareness down into your body so you can release your thinking mind. Free movement can take on a variety of forms. Perhaps you simply move a hand in response to music today, or maybe you dance in your imagination. Be gentle with yourself.

Sit down to your art journal or sheet of blank paper.

Decide whether music would support your drawing process or if silence works better. Part of what we're doing here is setting up conditions for you to notice how to trust and support yourself.

Draw a circle on the page either with a compass or with the bottom of a jar. As you draw this circle, let it be an act of prayer. You are creating a mandala or sacred container for your art-making. Placing the circle on the page is an act of commitment to yourself, to creating this space within where you can let whatever is moving through you come forth. You are creating the container—or tabernacle—for this time.

Connect again to your breath, and invite the Holy Spirit to be active in this process. Call on the wisdom of Hildegard of Bingen. Ask yourself: How can I best support my body's nourishment? Hold this question lightly.

Begin to explore images and symbols through color and shape. Using markers, colored pencils, or crayons, notice which colors are drawing you to them at this time without judgment or expectation. Thoughts such as *I always pick that color* or *I never pick that color* may come to mind; just be with them and see if you can focus on your breath and let them go, returning only to the process. Draw images or symbols or simply express something through coloring; it doesn't have to look like anything in particular.

Be fully aware of the process. Notice what thoughts or feelings arise. This is art as meditation, so we are cultivating our inner witness through this process. The witness is that calm, compassionate, curious, and infinitely wise part of ourselves that can observe what is happening internally without getting hooked by it. Remember that this isn't about making beautiful art but about being true to what is happening inside of you. We are cultivating the habit of not censoring ourselves and of noticing what is arising and letting it have space.

Once you come to a place of completion with your piece, let yourself have a few moments to sit in stillness. Let go of all thoughts and awareness for a brief time, and just rest into a space of being rather than doing.

Then move into a time of brief journaling and reflection. Spend a few minutes writing about what you noticed in this experience: What inner voices did you encounter, and what were the challenges and moments of ease? You are not trying to analyze your creation but to tend to the process, name what happened, and remain curious about your experience. Resist the urge to "figure out what it means"; rather, sit with the intuitive language of the body's expression. What did you discover?

Responses to Viriditas

My body is a poem. Clunky. Unattended.
    Untouched. Lonely and longing.
Enough? Too much?
Too much flesh. Too little movement.
My jeans getting tighter. My mind and
    intention drifting away.
"Move me, please," beg my hips. "Please
    move me."
I long to be moved and touched and
    pursued,
but I am a bottomless pit, wanting more
    and more . . .
And so, I eat more and drink more and
    move less
Instead of offering and pouring myself
    out for others and myself.

I am enough—just as I am—Enough.
I want to be moved . . . So move!
I want to be pursued . . . So pursue!
I want to be loved . . . So love!

This is my body psalm.

—Kayce Stevens Hughlett

I am Green, Viriditas, the greening of
    renewal, the thrusting new.

I am Red, the Life Force, pulsing,
    pulsing, beating, laughing, shouting,
    skipping joy.
I am Yellow, Light Within, warming,
    loving, shining brightly in the world.
I am Purple, Healing, wholeness, resting,
    holy softness, fragrant serenity.
Judith,
Rest in me and love me. Live in me and
    with me.
Let me love you, carry you, accompany
    you.
No need to tame or shame any longer.
Relish, rather, our relationship as
    companions on the Way—
Shimmering, shining, surely, steadily
Steadfast friends now and always.

—Judith Bryan

Library of Ferns

Embryos unfurling, stretching to prehistoric patterns. The forest light filtering through your serrations, the unfossilised, fresh-fronded teeth of pure unsullied green. Here is a nursery unravelling then, millions of years of timeless tedium, edenic shapes, untouched touchstone of evolution, perfect pyramids emerging, ancient parchments unrolling to reveal your viriditas vellum, your undeterred, unchanged message. Only the wind rustling the unread pages.

—Keren Dibbens-Wyatt

Movement Exploration

Yin Yoga: Corpse Pose

One of the most important poses in yoga practice is called corpse pose, *savasana* in Sanskrit. This pose is meant to imply not a physical death but a death and release of the old parts of ourselves that are no longer needed. Sometimes we need to shed old ideas about who we are to enter into greater freedom. At the end of a session of yoga poses, corpse pose helps us move into a time of rest, release, and integration. I think of it as a physical sabbath. When I teach yoga classes, I encourage participants to move into this pose at any time during the practice when their bodies need some rest or support from the floor.

I encourage you to begin by simply lying down in relaxation for five minutes. Breathe deeply at first, and then return to a natural breath. Let your body release completely. Notice any places of tightness and holding; see if you can let go of the tension and just feel yourself held. This is a practice of being rather than doing.

Hand Dance

For this first movement experience I invite you into a form that comes from InterPlay, which is a practice of improvisational movement and storytelling. You can learn more about this practice at www.InterPlay. org.

You can engage this practice while either sitting or lying down. You also need to select some music that is about three or four minutes long and have it available for the time of movement. Perhaps you already have a piece that comes to mind.

Before you begin, take some time to center yourself, connect to your breath, and focus on your heart. Place your hand on your heart to make a physical connection. As you rest here, hold the image of viriditas and God's greening power in the world. Invite this image in to be present with you as you explore through movement.

With one hand in front, explore the space around you. Move your hand through the air in front of you. Try making smooth movements and then jerky ones. Next, try smooth and slow, and then jerky and fast. Create a shape with your hand, then another, and then another. Explore the boundaries of the space around you, seeing how far your hand can reach. Rest your hand somewhere on your body and feel that physical connection. Then rest your hand somewhere else and pause.

Play the song you have selected for this time. Allow this to be a time of moving meditation and discovery. Trust this process and try not to think it through. See how your hand wants to explore the space around you, and allow it to lead. Move just one hand or both. As you move, simply be aware of this greening that flows through you, and let the dance be a response to this energy alive in you. Follow where the greening leads you.

When the song comes to an end, rest your hand in a closing gesture for a few moments. Breathe and become present to whatever your body is experiencing in the moment without trying to change it. Then allow a little time to write down any reflections in your journal.

Response to the Hand Dance

> My hands—always working
> holding books,
> scrubbing pots,
> typing, typing,
> holding up, holding out,
> holding everything.

Drudges that long to be
spiders dreamweaving
shapeshifters
shapemakers
fluttering shadow artists
and prayer makers
multiarmed sacred dancers
snake charming
the body
grown stiff and
sullen
Wake up!
There is still time!

—Heather A. Diamond

A Note About Movement

I realize that inviting you into movement with a piece of music may bring up some strong feelings right away and perhaps some (or a lot!) of resistance. First, let me just say that this is okay and natural. I believe that one of the main reasons we resist movement or dance is that engaging our bodies taps into emotions stored in us, so we might break open a stream of grief or anger and feel a bit frightened of where it takes us. And yet one of the great gifts of movement is that it does open up these streams in us that have been blocked and sometimes manifest in physical pain and illness.

Allowing the feeling to come, breathing into it, and riding through it, you will come to see emotions as waves that rise and subside. We will explore this further in chapter 4. When we allow space for them in our being, we don't have to fear getting stuck there. Movement will naturally open up places of stored emotion, and so sometimes our resistance to movement has to do with fear of what will come up for us. Always begin with some deep, slow breathing and the intention of creating a welcoming inner space, and let yourself feel what comes. When we don't block the emotional response, feelings rise and fall in a natural rhythm, so you can witness them coming and going.

Always feel free to do any of this work with your eyes open, if closing your eyes creates too much of a sense of claustrophobia. Know that you are always directing your own experience and can respond to your own needs at any time.

If calling this "dance" is too difficult, consider just calling it movement or gesture prayer. Allow yourself time to respond to your body's impulse. What would it be like to listen in and see how your body wanted to move for a few moments? What would offer some opening? To return to our question, what would feel nourishing? If your body cracks and creaks while moving, welcome in those sounds without judgment. Practice radical hospitality with the whole of your experience.

Tell yourself you will move for just five minutes (or start with three if that is too daunting!) and then you can stop, but see what happens in that time. This is a slow and gentle process of awakening the body's natural hunger for movement. Also, you are most welcome to move in your imagination to begin. Put on a piece of music you love, close your eyes if that feels comfortable, and see yourself moving in whatever way your body longs to. There is actually research that shows this has a physical effect in your body and stimulates the system in positive ways. Grief may arise, but that is okay as well. Let it move through you.

Notice if you are telling yourself an old story. Do you tell yourself you don't dance because of messages that you don't have the body of a dancer, or do you fear looking foolish? (This is where dancing in the privacy of your own space can open up possibilities and experimentation.) Most of us have old wounds that inhibit our possibilities for movement; the invitation is to listen into this moment now without getting stuck in the past—what does the body long for? And know this will be different from day to day, sometimes moment to moment.

Reflection Questions

At the end of each chapter I include some questions for reflection. These can be responded to through journaling or meditating on them and seeing what responses arise. They are meant to be evocative and to open up new possibilities for the journey.

- What are you discovering about what nourishes you and what depletes you?
- In what ways do you tend to flee your inner experience?
- How might you invite the gift of greenness into your body each day?
- What is your relationship to body movement? If it feels difficult, can you offer yourself some grace and compassion as you move slowly?

Closing Blessing

Each chapter will close with a blessing, a "BodyPsalm" written by Celeste Snowber. Celeste is a professor of arts education in Vancouver, British Columbia, who studies embodiment. I have loved Celeste's creative work for many years. A psalm is an ancient prayer from the Hebrew Scriptures that evokes a wide range of human emotion. These contemporary psalms invite us into another way to honor the body's experience.

As we begin this journey together, here is a psalm for new beginnings.

BodyPsalm for Body Beginnings

Each day the petals
unfold their face to the sky
an act of surrender
open hearted to breathe
for a new day
Await each breath as if it was pristine
your lungs living in the glory of
inhabiting air for the first time
everything is old today
everything is new today
all your issues remain
family, finances, relationships, work details, and
endless domestic disasters

but there is a spring
rising within your torso
you know it by its pulse
the energy where you cry yes
to this tiny alive moment
let the morning birds sing inside your chest
and cultivate body beginnings
new ways for fingers to touch earth
glances for being a lover in the world
finding ease through baby steps
the big deals—the big problems
will be with you
but there is something else arising
a ripe heart—a softened soul
an eternal arm embraces your weariness
and calls you back once again
to body beginnings.

—Celeste Snowber

Chapter 2

Breath:
The Gateway to the Body

[God's] breath vibrates in yours, in your voice. It is the breath of God that you breathe—and you are unaware of it.

—Theophilus of Antioch

In the first creation story of Genesis, the scene begins with the earth as a formless void and the wind of the Divine sweeping over the waters. In the second creation story, God is described as gathering mud and clay from the earth and then breathing the first breath of life to create human beings. From these stories of our beginnings we are given insight into a Creator whose very nature is intimately connected to wind and breath. We are animated and enlivened by the breath that is breathed into us.

The prophet Ezekiel tells the story of the dry bones that are brought back to life by being renewed with flesh and then breathed into to animate them again. In the gospels, Jesus breathes on the disciples (Jn 20:21–22), and at Pentecost the Spirit comes as a mighty wind (Acts 2:1–4). All three persons of the Trinity are woven together by this element of air.

It is clear that breath is considered part of the fundamental nature of God. As human beings, our breath sustains us moment by moment, even when we are completely unaware. We can consciously deepen our breathing, but our breath will continue on until our last one. The great

Jesuit theologian Teilhard de Chardin has a wonderful image of the "breathing together of all things." All living creatures are sustained by this life-giving rhythm, and we are dependent on plants, trees, and other vegetation to transform the carbon dioxide we exhale into the oxygen we need to thrive.

It All Begins with Breath

> The soul that is united and transformed in God breathes
> God in God with the same divine breathing with which
> God, while in her, breathes her in himself.
>
> —St. John of the Cross

Pause just a moment before reading further to notice your breath without trying to change it. Track your breathing for a few moments, bringing a sense of wonder to this primal rhythm that sustains your life even when you aren't paying attention, such as while you are sleeping, eating, or in deep conversation with a dear friend. The breath, like the heartbeat, is the ancient rhythm and pulse of life. The breath is like an old and loyal friend with whom you are becoming reacquainted.

Imagine, for a moment, the story of creation from the book of Genesis, where it says that God breathed life into that lump of clay to create a human being, a living soul. Breath is what animates us. Imagine that God sustains your breath moment by moment as sheer gift.

In Hebrew and Latin the words for "breath" are *ruach* and *spiritus*, respectively, both of which also mean "spirit." Our spiritual ancestors knew this connection between breath and the Divine. This is the incarnation—to know God as intimately moving through our physical being. The breath is a beautiful place to begin with this awareness.

Call on the image Theophilus and John of the Cross offer to us above, that it is the very breath of God that you breathe. Every breath is a gateway into awareness of the body, giving presence to its needs and longings.

The breath can be controlled and deepened. When you find yourself becoming anxious or fretful, when you feel as though you are grasping at life rather than receiving what comes, slow down your breath to remind yourself of the spaciousness that is possible within. Breathing slowly also has a physical effect of relaxing the body. To invite spaciousness is to consciously direct the breath to places that feel tight and constricted in order to intentionally soften and expand them. This is an ongoing practice to cultivate rather than a one-time result.

Yogic tradition offers many beautiful ways to practice working with the breath. There is breath to raise the energy, breath to relax, the breath of joy, and breath for balance. *Pranayama*, breathing practices in the ancient yogic path, are just as vital as the *asanas*, the physical poses.

Breath was also central to the practice of the desert monks. We have texts that describe their practice of the Jesus Prayer, where the breath is slowed and a prayer is said in coordination. Usually the first part—"Lord Jesus Christ, Son of God"—was said on the inhale, and the second part—"have mercy on me, a sinner"—was said while exhaling. Praying with each breath was one of the ways they could "pray without ceasing" (1 Thes 5:16).

Women who have gone through labor know that the breath is an essential ally in bearing the pain of labor and easing the body's burden. When we hold the breath we create strain on our system. When we work with the breath in intentional ways, we open up space within us. Breath can support us in laboring of all kinds—including the emotional pains of grief or anger as well as physical pain—and a deep sigh can open up an experience of pleasure and release.

Breath as Anchor and Grounding

> The lungs know this secret as well as any can know it: that the inward and the outward depths partake of the same mystery, that as the unseen wind swirls within us, so it also whirls all around us, bending the grasses and lofting the clouds even as it lights our own sensations.
>
> —David Abram, *Becoming Animal*

Our breath is an incredibly powerful tool for coming to physical awareness of our bodies.

Holding our breath or breathing shallowly is connected to our bodies going into survival mode. The sympathetic nervous system is activated, which floods our bodies with hormones to prepare to fight, flight, or freeze. When we are chronically in this heightened state, our bodies suffer.

When we practice regular, natural, and full diaphragmatic breaths, we open our bodies to a different way of being, activating our parasympathetic nervous system, one rooted not in survival concerns but in a sense of calm and being centered.

Conscious breathing helps to interrupt the survival response that increases our stress and anxiety. Learning to breathe deeply and slowly helps to relieve anxiety and calm our nervous systems. While we are mostly unable to control our heartbeat, digestive system, and hormonal release, we can consciously direct the breath to calm the whole body, which in turn affects all of these systems in positive ways. For those suffering from trauma, the breath becomes an anchor to the present moment. Instead of allowing a trigger to lead to shallow breathing, we can consciously practice ways of slowing everything down, breaking this cycle of shallow breathing leading to stress and anxiety that causes more shallow breathing.

You can extend this experience even further by imagining when you inhale that you draw the breath up through your feet and through your body, and then exhale in the same manner. Imagine that when you breathe in you are drawing in nourishment and support from the earth. When you exhale, imagine sending roots deep down. This can have a grounding effect. Anytime we start to feel disconnected, directing our awareness to our feet with our breath can bring us back to the present moment. While we can't literally breathe into our feet, we can direct our attention and awareness in such a way that our breath becomes a threshold to deepened awareness.

Statio: Breath as Holy Pause

Every breath is a resurrection.

—Gregory Orr,
"Concerning the Book That Is the Body of the Beloved"

In the monastic tradition there is a practice called *statio*, which is the commitment to stop one thing before beginning another. Imagine that instead of rushing from one appointment to the next you pause between each one and breathe just five long, slow breaths. Imagine how this might transform your movement from one activity to another. Or even when you move from one room to another, allow a brief pause on the threshold between spaces. God lives inside our breath, and so every breath can become a resurrection.

For the Celtic monks, thresholds were sacred places. The space or the moment between—whether physical places or experiences—is a place of possibility. Rather than waiting being a nuisance or arriving with a sense that you are wasting time, the pause at a threshold is an invitation to breathe into the now and receive its gifts.

Each moment of the breath is a threshold—the movement from inhale to fullness to exhale to emptiness. The breath can help us stay present to all of the moments of transition in our lives when we feel tempted to rush breathlessly to the next thing. Instead of rushing, what happens in our bodies and hearts when we intentionally pause? When we honor this threshold as sacred? When we breathe deeply and slowly for even a single minute?

Statio calls us to a sense of reverence for slowness and mindfulness. We can open up a space within for God to work. We can become fully conscious of what we are about to do rather than mindlessly starting and completing another task. We call upon the breath as an ancient soul friend to help us witness our lives unfolding rather than being carried along until we aren't sure where our lives are going. We can return again and again to our bodies and their endless wisdom and listen at every threshold.

We often think of these in-between times as wasted moments and inconveniences rather than as opportunities to return again and again to the expansiveness of the present moment and the body's opening to us right now. Our invitation is to awaken to the gifts right here, not the ones we imagine waiting for us beyond the next door.

Sensation and Body Wisdom

> For the Spirit shall go forth from me,
> and I have made every breath.
>
> —Isaiah 57:16[1]

The breath can also be a tremendous gift in learning how to access and pay attention to body sensations. We can use the breath to help draw our awareness from the place it usually rests, somewhere in the head and often between the eyes, and let it descend down into the body, usually in the heart center or gut. The breath becomes a tool of awareness and focus for tending to the sensations that arise in the body.

One of the ways we can directly access the beauty of the incarnation is through attending to bodily sensation. Sensation is a language of our physical selves. We experience sensation all the time in our bodies, but largely we are not attuned to those sensations. Breathing helps to slow us down, descend into the experience of our bodies, and notice what arises. Sensations may come as feelings or images, as felt senses of things. They often rise and fall, so one of the gifts of turning inward to witness them is seeing how sensations often move like waves, rising and falling when an experience feels intense.

When we move into yoga poses, we are essentially working with the three tools of breath, shape, and sensation. The shape is the actual form the pose takes in our bodies, breath brings our awareness to the present moment, and sensation is the experience we have while in the pose.

Breath becomes our ally on the descent into the wilderness of the body. I love wilderness as a metaphor for our encounter with our bodies because we are often very unfamiliar with the terrain and may fear getting lost or unearthing painful feelings. But the wilderness is also a place of profound renewal and connection to a part of ourselves we tend to forget in our everyday experience. Spending time there can release a tremendous amount of healing energy as we rediscover the grace of our embodied selves.

The desert elders would go out into the wilderness as a way to encounter God beyond their own preconceived ideas. They went to free themselves of patterns and habits of thinking and being that kept them imprisoned. The body offers us this freedom and holy encounter if we make the descent willingly, even if a bit reluctantly.

When we practice deep breathing, we can imagine ourselves descending into the terrain of the body, and from there we can begin to cultivate the capacity to listen to our body sensations and the wisdom they may be offering. We so rarely take the time to just sit still and listen to what our bodies are saying that this can be a revelatory moment in itself.

Sometimes we may descend with the breath and our imagination, and feel frustrated that our bodies don't seem to be speaking or aren't saying what we want to hear. This is where patience and commitment are required. Our bodies don't speak in linear ways. It takes time to grow more fluent in the language of sensation and to learn what they are telling us. This is the place to begin.

Ally on the Journey: Sophia as Holy Wisdom

> For she is a breath of the power of God, and a pure emanation of the glory of the Almighty.
>
> —Wisdom 7:25–26

The Hebrew Scriptures have many descriptions of the figure of Wisdom or Sophia, which is the Greek translation of her name. She is always depicted as feminine and here is imagined as the very breath of God. This connects her to the Holy Spirit in the Christian Trinity because the words for spirit and breath, as we discussed earlier, are the same in both Latin (*spiritus*) and Hebrew (*ruach*).

As we gather allies for this healing journey, imagine Sophia here with you as a presence and a power of the Divine. She breathes through you and all things, making her as intimate as your very breath. Pause and invite her to breathe through you, holding this image of her presence as the very power of the Divine.

Ask for her support and guidance in this process of deepening into the wisdom of the breath. Know that with every inhale and exhale, she permeates your being, supporting you and enlivening you.

Practice: Yielding and the Invitation to Soften

Surrender / Against Beloved's luminous breath

—Hafiz, "The Gift"

The breath is connected intimately to our bodies by bringing oxygen to our blood that nourishes our whole system. When we breathe slowly and deeply, we initiate a physical response counter to the shallow and anxious breath with which we usually move through life. Breathing in this intentional way has an effect on our bodies.

One very simple way to slow down and bring more ease to your breath is to find a comfortable position and then breathe in for a count of four and then out for a count of four, letting the breath become slow and steady. It can also be helpful to put your hands on your belly and consciously deepen your breath so that your belly rises. This happens when our breathing is full and expands the diaphragm. Once this kind of breathing becomes more natural, we can also bring the breath to places of tension and holding. Breath is a way for us to physically practice surrender rather than control.

One of my favorite body practices is yin yoga, in which seated poses targeting spine and hips are held for three to five minutes. In that span of time I can begin to notice the places of physical holding in my body. I breathe deeply and bring my breath to these areas of tension. The breath helps me to soften these places, and over time in the pose, I witness myself going deeper, even if only slightly.

When I intentionally soften the places where my body feels tight, something remarkable happens. Softening the body supports me in softening my mind, so my thoughts feel less grasping and more at peace. My eyes soften, and I can look at the world with a softer gaze, open to receiving the gifts before me. My heart softens, allowing space for feeling and emotion to pass through, rather than cutting myself off from this river of life. Body, mind, and heart are intimately connected to each other. When we carry tension in one place, it shows up in the others, so this practice works on many layers and levels.

Carry this awareness with you throughout the coming days. When you feel tense or rushed, pause and notice if you are holding your body anywhere, acknowledge where you feel tightness, and simply bring your breath to that place and be mindful of what happens. Imagine that the Spirit breathes the breath of life into you, and as you breathe out you release your body even more. We carry so much body armor; our breath helps to soften those places, opening them up to our awareness.

Meditation: Create Your Own Breath Prayer

Kabir says: Student, tell me, what is God? / He is the breath inside the breath.

—Kabir

I mentioned earlier the traditional Jesus Prayer used by the desert elders for staying in a state of continual prayer and presence. Feel free to use these words if they feel nourishing as you connect to your breath, but my invitation to you is to create your own breath prayer.

Allow a few minutes to quiet and listen to your body. Let your breath be gentle and slow, and see if you can connect with the prayer your body wants to offer. What is the longing that rises up from your body when you sit in stillness?

It might be something simple such as

> Breathing in: "I breathe in greenness," or
>   "I welcome *viriditas*"
> Breathing out: "I breathe out dryness," or
>   "I release *ariditas*"

Or it might be something such as

> Breathing in: "Grant me nourishment"
> Breathing out: "in every moment"

You might connect your breath prayer to a scripture verse such as one from the Psalms.

> Breathing in: "Be still and know"
> Breathing out: "that I am God" (Ps 46:10)

Or

> Breathing in: "Let everything that
>   breathes"
> Breathing out: "praise God" (see Ps
>   150:6)

Or it might be a single word on each inhale and exhale. Let the prayer become your own. What would be most nourishing?

Responses to the Breath Prayer

> Breathe in: "I open the door to my heart"
> Breathe out: "I release what I am holding
>   too tight"

—Ellen Ratmeyer

> Breathe in possibility
> Breathe out limitation

Breathe in openness
Breathe out release

Unfold my path
before me

—Heather A. Diamond

Breathe in me—breath of Life
Breathe in me—breath of Light
Breathe in me—breath of Love
Breathe in me—breath of Healing
Breathe in me—breath of Peace

—Cindy Read

Make the prayer your own. See what calls to you as a way to stay connected to your body's own deep longing. I recommend keeping it under eight words. Allow a day or two to see what your prayer might be. Once you have let it chosen you, pray with it over several days and see what you notice or discover.

The desert elders would engage the breath as a way to descend into the body and the space around the heart, which for them was the center of our being. The rhythm of the breath connects us to the other ancient rhythm of the heartbeat. When we slow down enough to hear both, we are plunged into the body's pulse and music. Listen to that song.

Once you have settled into your prayer, make a commitment to sit for five minutes each morning breathing and offering this prayer with every inhale and exhale. When you remember during the day, pause for just a few seconds to say the prayer again so that it becomes a thread weaving throughout your day. I also encourage you to simply sit and breathe without words sometimes. The silence offers an invitation to cross the threshold into the body, and the breath becomes your gateway.

Creative Exploration: Poem Writing

One of my favorite lines of poetry comes from Mary Oliver's poem "Have You Ever Tried to Enter the Long Black Branches?" She writes, "Listen, are you breathing just a little, and calling it a life?" There is so much wrapped up in that question. It is one to ponder and live into, to gently and slowly begin to unfurl the places in our lives where we are wound too tightly.

One way to write a poem is to take the line of another poem as your starting point. I invite you to write this question from Mary Oliver across the top of a piece of paper and then, in a free write, a spontaneous exploration, write anything that comes to mind in response. This is a time not for editing but for a free flow of ideas. If it is less intimidating to think of it as a journal entry, begin there.

Then set the paper aside for a day and come back to it. Begin to remove words that aren't essential, and divide the lines so they create natural pauses in the rhythm of reading them. You might write your poem in a body journal as a reminder of the gift of breath.

Here are some examples:

> "Listen, are you breathing just a little,
>   and calling it a life?"
> Is that supposed to be a question? A little
>   is better than nothing.
> What if it is all I have?
> Sometimes the tide is small and gentle
> Sometimes the sand can be kissed lightly
> And still the grains are wet, and shore is
>   shore.
> Would I be a better person
> Were I able to run and jump and take
> Great lungfuls of the stuff of life?
> Maybe my expansion comes in other
>   ways
> Not just bodily swellings,

But in the sending out of shoots from
    this darkness
Into the loam that takes breath for me,
And tender leaves above to exhale.

—Keren Dibbens-Wyatt

"Listen, are you breathing just a little,
and calling it a life?"

Listen, just a little breath
quick, incomplete, chest-tight
mind-full, heart-silent.

Listen, a little breath
Is air scarce? Do I need to ration it
for a rainy day, a day when I will
need it more?

Listen, little breaths
Is air too precious, too extravagant
to be savored each moment,
deeply, fully?

Listen, deep breaths
Drawing in the overflowing
abundance of God
each breath life
each breath sacred
each breath union.

Listen.

—Marilyn Yeager

"Listen,
are you breathing just a little, and calling
   it a life?"

Observe the birds, they sing, they fly.
And flowers bloom, then willingly die.

Are you willing to die to old habits so as
to be resurrected again, and again, and
   again?

—Audrey Stromberg

Movement Exploration

Yin Yoga: Butterfly

butterfly

I invite you to add some yin yoga to your movement practice. As with all movement practice, you make modifications for your body and your needs. We never strive to have a practice that looks like someone else's. That is our ego talking.

As I have mentioned, from a physical perspective, yin yoga is a practice of holding poses (mostly seated poses that focus on the hips and spine) for three to five minutes as a way of targeting connective tissue beneath the muscles. When you move into a yin pose, you allow a few moments to find the place at the edge of sensation, but you should never feel pain in the pose. Props can be used for support; there should never be straining to hold a pose. If you are having trouble breathing, you are in the pose too far. If you feel pain of any kind, come out of the pose.

Because you are working the connective tissue rather than the muscles, you actually want to do this practice with the muscles cold. It can be helpful to set a timer with a gentle ring or chime while holding the pose so you do not have to watch the clock.

As you hold a pose, stay connected to your breath and bring your breath to any places of holding or tension to allow softening to happen. Yin yoga is very much a practice of paying attention, yielding, and cultivating stillness as opposed to a more yang practice of striving for active, muscular poses. We live in a very yang culture, so the yin practice invites us into softening and yielding in our bodies and minds. In yin we practice an attitude of allowing and accepting whatever is true for us in this moment and then bringing the breath in service of our continued softening in body, mind, and thoughts.

Something very interesting happens as we sit and breathe in this place that is just at the edge of discomfort for three minutes or longer: We have a chance to be with our minds and the chatter of our thoughts. We start to notice this relentless narrative and commentary about how we have so much to do, why are we wasting our time, why can't we stretch farther, how much longer is there to go, and so on. And we can bring our breath to our minds and our thoughts and invite them to soften, just the way we do with our muscles.

We can also be present to the rise and fall of our feelings in this practice. Because we are working with the body, and because many yin poses target the hips that tend to hold a lot of emotion, feelings may arise. The hips and pelvic bowl hold our sexual organs, and some of us may hold shame here about our sexual experiences as well as previous trauma. This is a perfect time to practice allowing your emotions through your body, an exercise we will explore further in chapter 4. Let your breath soften your heart so that you can let go of resistance.

My suggestion is to begin with just one yin posture each day and hold it for three minutes. There are many possible poses, but one of my favorite places to begin is the butterfly pose. It is also known as the bound angle pose in more traditional yoga practice. The yin poses are largely the same ones you practice in a more yang-style class, but they are held longer and have softer, gentler names to reinforce the motivation behind the practice.

Come to seated position and bring the soles of your feet together with your knees bent outward. Your heels might be close to your groin or far away, whatever works for your body. Take a nice deep breath, and round your spine down and over your legs as far as you can comfortably go. It might be just a little bit. You can use props under your knees and even a bolster to support your head if that feels helpful.

Bernie Clark is a yin yoga teacher and trainer in Vancouver, British Columbia, and has an excellent website, www.YinYoga.com, with many videos to introduce you to this practice. I highly recommend finding the corresponding poses on his website and watching both the teaching and demonstration for each pose when available. If his website does not have a particular pose, you can search on YouTube for other demonstrations.

As you hold the pose, soften your body, your thoughts, and your heart, allowing your breath to be your anchor. Let these three minutes be a container for your own awareness. Gently become aware if there is a desire rising up in you, and allow space for that to be as well. If three minutes feels fairly easy, you could try remaining in the pose for four or five minutes, but be cautious and discern if this is your ego's desire or your body's desire. This is not a competition. See what feels most nourishing.

Come out of your yin yoga pose very gently and slowly. Allow a few moments to gently rock your legs, arch your back gently to release the spine, or do anything else that would feel good. Imagine yourself a butterfly emerging from her cocoon. You can close with a return to *savasana* or corpse pose from our first chapter. This is a way for the body to have a moment to integrate the practice.

Dancing with the Breath

Your invitation is to enter into movement through the breath. Put on a piece of flute music, which is music of the breath. If you don't have any yourself, you can do an online search.

I invite you to integrate softening, stability, and *statio* into this movement. Begin with several long, slow breaths. Play the flute music, but don't start moving right away. Pause first, practicing this monastic *statio*, aware that you are on the threshold between stillness and moving.

As you feel the impulse to move arising in your body, follow it. It may be as simple as raising your arms on the inhale and lowering them on the exhale. Let the movement be very slow and mindful so that you remain present to the experience. Let this be a time of exploring the vow of stability by staying fully with yourself; whenever your attention drifts, simply bring it back to this moment. Feel free to pause whenever you need to.

Notice places in your body that feel tight with tension, and bring your breath there. Perhaps make some slow circles to open the space there.

After several minutes of moving meditation, staying present to yourself, and listening as well as you can to your body's impulses and following them, pause again. Notice the energy moving through your body and any shifts from when you first began.

Reflection Questions

- Where are you breathing only as much as necessary and calling it fully living?
- How is the breath calling you into deeper intimacy with your body and the divine presence that sustains you?
- How does the breath invite you into a journey of yielding to grace?

- Check in with yourself: How are you doing? Are you being gentle with yourself? If not, can you return ever so gently to the place of witnessing, tending, and discovering? Remember that this is a life-long journey, so there is no need to be somewhere other than where you are.

Closing Blessing

Body Psalm for Grace

Know there is a flow
working within the vessels
of your life and blood
through each spiritual artery and vein
which has a current all to its own

you cannot stop the life stream
only enhance its surge
listen for the sound
of grace inhabiting
the map of your path

let what is unseen carry you
in its crest and
give into the wave
of the ebb and flow
of your own pulse

who knows where your journey will lead
or what you may discover
you are in a new chapter
of your own autobiography
rewriting your own narrative
every moment you take a breath

Let the air breathe you
and allow the mist of the unpredictable
to caress your own plans
widen your embrace
of what is possible
it is in the impossible
where grace
will have her way
and find you once again
with an open heart
to touch the sky
and inhabit your dreams.

Celeste Snowber

Chapter 3

Senses:
The Threshold and
Sacrament of Experience

As the twelfth-century teacher Hildegard of Bingen
says, "God has a burning love for the flesh." And there
are four stages, she says, in the ascent of holy knowing:
"seeing, hearing, smelling, and tasting."

—J. Philip Newell,
A New Harmony

The Catholic Mass, which is my own home tradition, is often described as "smells and bells." A full liturgy will often meet and inspire every one of our senses: smelling rising incense, hearing bells ring, viewing stained-glass windows, singing songs, embracing one another at the kiss of peace, eating the bread, and drinking wine.

I have always loved the Catholic idea of sacramentality, which means that physical things participate in and reveal the presence of the holy. The liturgy with all of its sensual dimensions is sacramental, the marriage union between two lovers is sacramental, the holy oil of anointing used in healing is sacramental, and this bread and wine that become flesh and blood are sacramental.

And then there are the more ordinary, everyday sacraments. Awakening to a new day and pausing to savor a cup of tea is sacramental. Feeling overwhelming gratitude when a friend shows up for me in my time of grief is sacramental. And giving myself the gift of a Sabbath day of rest and renewal is sacramental. The sacramentality of our own flesh allows us to be present in this world and receive its gifts through our senses.

If we ponder the monastery setting, we might imagine the soaring arches of the cloisters, the fragrant garden in the center providing herbs and medicine for healing and a taste of Eden in their midst, and the songs rising at the hours for prayer. There is a profound honoring of the way these sensual delights can bring us closer to God.

To have a sacramental spirituality is to honor that our senses are doorways into the holy. When we bring ourselves intentionally to an experience and let ourselves receive it through our senses, the richness of it and the multidimensionality of it shimmer forth.

There is even a tradition in Christian spirituality of what are called the "spiritual senses." The senses were seen as so essential to receiving the gift of the sacred in the world that there was believed to be parallel interior senses to the exterior ones. There was spiritual vision, which was the ability to see God beneath the surface of things. There was spiritual hearing, which was the capacity to hear God underneath the noises and distractions. Each sense, including taste, smell, and touch, was imagined as having these inner counterparts and, when cultivated, offering us the ability to encounter God in the flesh-and-blood reality of the world.

The Call to Savor

> Only by welcoming uncertainty from the get-go can we acclimate ourselves to the shattering wonder that enfolds us. This animal body, for all its susceptibility and vertigo, remains the primary instrument of all our knowing, as the capricious earth remains our primary cosmos.
>
> —David Abram, *Becoming Animal*

When I was a young girl, my parents often called me "the sensual child" because I was always so taken with tastes and textures, smells and sounds. Children often have this uninhibited connection to the world. This way of savoring the world has continued into my adulthood, but with the busyness of life I have to be more intentional in my savoring. It is so easy to let myself be carried by the rush of life and miss the delights of embodied life or to become self-conscious about relishing the delights of pleasure.

One of my favorite poets is Rainer Maria Rilke. A central motivation of his poetry is to explore what it means to live *this* human life we are given and to discover the inner nature of *my* particular experience, knowing that this familiar life and body will not ever come again.

This life and body with which I wrestle but have also grown so fond of and familiar with are not permanent. I had an encounter with the stark reality of my own mortality in 2010 when I was hospitalized with a pulmonary embolism while traveling alone in Vienna, and that experience thrust me into a far more intense appreciation for everything in my life, as often happens following a near-death experience.

As I ponder this reality, a phrase begins to form: "savor this life and this body." Then a question begins to shimmer: What if the meaning of my life is to experience my particular life, my unique body, my lens on the world, and my encounters with grief and loss, delight and joy, all as my unique story never to be repeated again? What might I discover by remembering this daily? How might my relationship to my own experience and to this wondrous vessel that carries me through it all be transformed if I not just offer gratitude for my life but also savor it with relish, knowing that this moment will never again happen? What if I were to honor my senses as the sacred thresholds that bring me into communion with the gift that I am in the world? What if I were to trust that *this* moment carries profound wisdom I need to transform my service to the world?

The winter days following my hospitalization with my beloved husband who rushed from the United States to be by my side were incredibly sweet and rich. We walked hand in hand through parks with bare trees, so grateful to be together and alive; again I found myself deeply in love with this man, and I savored the feel of his rough skin against mine. I savored his gaze over me, so full of love and familiarity. I savored the way his breath made a faint cloud with each exhale on that chilly evening. Food tasted all the more incredible and music so full of sweetness and longing at this time.

Out of this near encounter with death arose a sense of urgency for me in my life. The things I had wanted to do someday, such as live overseas, suddenly became much more important to pay attention to now. It was certainly part of the impetus to finally move to Europe a couple of years later as we had longed to do.

The root of the word *savor* comes from the Latin word *saporem*, which means "to taste" and is also the root of *sapient*, which is the word for "wisdom." Another definition I love is "to give oneself over to the enjoyment of something." When I give myself over to the experience of savoring, wisdom emerges. Savoring calls for a kind of surrender. We have all kinds of stories in our minds about why we shouldn't give ourselves over to enjoyment, whether out of guilt, shame, or a sense of fear of what might happen. Yet we are called to yield to the goodness of life, to bask in it. It is an affirmation and celebration of God's creation and an echo of "it is good" from Genesis.

Savoring calls me to slowness: I can't savor quickly.

Savoring calls me to spaciousness: I can't savor everything at once.

Savoring calls me to mindfulness: I can't savor without being fully present.

Savoring also calls for a fierce and wise discernment about how I spend my time and energy. Now that I know deep in my bones the limits of my life breaths, how do I choose to spend those dazzling hours? What experiences ripening within me long for exploration? Do I want to waste my time skating on the surface of things, in a breathless rush to get everything done when all I need is here in this moment?

There is also a seasonal quality to savoring—this season, what is right before me right now, is to be savored. It will rise and fall, come into fullness and then slip away. When I savor I pay attention to all the moments of that experience without trying to force it to change.

There is a tremendous sweetness to this openhearted way of being in the world. Everything becomes grace because I recognize it could all be different; it could all be gone. Rather than grasp at how I think this moment *should* be, I savor the way things *are*.

Song of Songs

> Let us go out early to the vineyards,
> and see whether the vines have budded,
> whether the grape blossoms have opened
> and the pomegranates are in bloom.
> There I will give you my love.

—Song of Songs 7:12

I love not only that the Song of Songs exists in the Bible but also that the ancient rabbis called it the Holy of Holies. The medieval monks were fascinated by this text as well. Bernard of Clairvaux—that famous monk of the twelfth century who lived at the same time as Hildegard of Bingen and helped support her visions and give her authority—was the primary builder of the Cistercian order, which was a reform of the Benedictines to return to greater simplicity and the roots of their practice.

Bernard reemphasized the essential nature of lectio divina. He famously wrote *Sermons on the Song of Songs* out of his own practice of lectio divina. He wrote eighty-six sermons and still did not complete the whole book; there was so much richness he discovered there. As a celibate monk he emphasized the Song as an allegory for our desire for God, for the passion we are called to experience in our spirituality. I think the biblical text functions on both levels: it is an earthly celebration of the goodness and mutuality of sexual love and sensual experience, and at the same time, it speaks to our heart's deepest desire for the divine presence. In both ways of reading the text, the senses become a threshold to a sacred encounter.

One of my favorite books is *Exquisite Desire: Religion, the Erotic, and the Song of Songs* by Carey Ellen Walsh, an exploration of the Song of Songs. In it, Walsh writes, "What this Song does, and unabashedly, is champion a passion for life itself." She suggests that the book itself was an erotic love poem, and by its inclusion in the Bible, "its theme experientially resonates for the reader on both the sexual and spiritual planes."[1]

Jesus as a Sensual Man

We have another ally in this quest to learn to savor life with our senses, Jesus himself. When we read stories from the gospels with our senses alert, we encounter Jesus immersed in a whole array of sensual experiences. Table fellowship was a primary way of marking significant events in the Bible. In the Gospel of Luke, there are ten stories alone that refer to times Jesus sat down to a meal with others, often with those on the margins.[2] Jesus is criticized for not being selective enough. Everyone is welcome to feast with him; you don't have to be rich enough, smart enough, or thin enough to do so.

He is concerned with making sure people are fed, and as in the story of the multiplication of loaves and fishes, there is even an excess left over, as if to reinforce that there is always more than enough. Jesus' first miracle was turning water into wine at the wedding feast to make sure the party was able to continue. His final ritual act with his disciples was to break bread and pour wine as his own Body and Blood. The way he reached out to others was through earthy pleasures of nourishment.

In all four of the gospels we have the story of the woman who anointed Jesus with expensive perfume and washed his feet with her tears. In the Gospel of Luke, she is referred to as a "harlot." The Pharisee in the story criticizes Jesus: Does he know what kind of woman this is? In the other stories, the objection revolves around the waste. Despite the label given to her that would relegate her to the shadows of her culture, she is bold and steps forward, caring little about what others think of her; she follows her sense of call to perform this act of extravagance, this act of grace and love. Jesus rejects that her generosity is too much, that anything has been wasted. "She has performed a good service for me," he insists (Mk 14:6).

Somehow many of us are taught early on not to be too extravagant, too indulgent, or too *much*. We are taught to hold back and that indulging ourselves in sensual pleasure is somehow suspect rather than a portal to the deepest kind of prayer—the one where we discover the holiness in embracing someone we love, enjoying a meal prepared with care, inhaling the fragrance of basil and thyme, walking through the forest and smelling the earth and pine, or feeling the spray of salt water standing by the sea. Holiness is not some disconnected, disembodied journey. What does it mean to believe that the journey to the heart of God and God's desires for me lies in the descent into the wilderness of my body even if I still have no idea how to go about that?

Ally on the Journey: The Woman from Song of Songs

> While the king was on his couch,
> my nard gave forth its fragrance.
> My beloved is to me a bag of myrrh
> that lies between my breasts.
> My beloved is to me a cluster of henna blossoms
> in the vineyards of En-gedi.
>
> —Song of Songs 1:12–14

You might imagine that joining you alongside Hildegard of Bingen with her reminder of viriditas and Sophia with her reminder of the gift of breath to connect with Spirit is the unnamed woman of the Song of Songs whose desire and lavish savoring of her beloved are laid open without embarrassment there in the scriptures.

She invites us to remember how very good the world can be and to savor it fully. Here is a woman who is in command of and enjoying her own sensual nature. Savoring and the senses are not just about sensuality, however. She witnesses to a way of being in the world that celebrates the goodness of creation as revelatory of life's sweetness.

Invite her in to support you in your own journey of learning to fall in love with all the ways the Divine is revealed through earthly things and delights.

Practice: Conversion and Letting Ourselves Be Surprised by God

In the first chapter we explored the monastic vow of stability: how it calls us to stay with our experience and not run away. Stability asks us to be present to our bodies with all of the feelings that arise and to notice them with compassion.

In this chapter we move into another monastic vow, which is conversion. The root of this practice is an acknowledgment that we are always on a journey. The contemplative has never arrived at completion. There is always more to learn.

Two aspects of this stand out for me, especially in relationship to this journey deeper into our bodies. First is the invitation of conversion to always be open to being surprised by God. Once cynicism has overshadowed us and we think we have seen or done it all and there is no possibility of redemption left, we have abandoned hope and the God of newness. For me, letting myself be surprised by the Divine means letting go of the story of the years of baggage I carry around about my relationship to my body and the ways I tell myself I will always fail or I will never be able to enter fully into my body's wisdom because of all this resistance I have. When I let these go, suddenly I have a moment of profound insight or connection. When I think I have heard it all before and suddenly I hear it in a new way—so it lands somewhere deeper, more solid—I can let myself be surprised by the Divine in another way. Conversion reminds me of the gift of holy surprise.

The second invitation of conversion, and perhaps even more important (and most hopeful), is the reminder that we always begin again. We are called to bring a beginner's mind to this process, knowing that we always have something new to learn. Each time I "fail" in my attempts to be mindful, to savor, and to cherish the sensual delights of a meal, for example, instead of berating myself for this act of forgetting, I begin again. Simply, with great compassion and without drama, I commit myself again to the path. Some days I will have strayed very far before I even realize I have left. Other days I will be in the middle of a meal and remember, *Oh yes, wasn't I going to be more present while I eat?* Conversion reminds me of the gift of new beginnings.

Two stories from the Desert Fathers and Mothers illustrate this principle:

> Abba Poemen said about Abba Pior that every single day he made a fresh beginning.[3]

> Abba Moses asked Abba Silvanus, "Can a man lay a new foundation every day?" The old man said, "If he works hard he can lay a new foundation at every moment."[4]

When it comes to our bodies, we perhaps are forever feeling like failures with our diets and exercise routines. Conversion calls us gently back, not by berating ourselves but as an act of love and loving attention to what is true in this moment. The new beginning is right here and now if we choose to open ourselves and stop living in regret and self-judgment.

Conversion also asks that we allow ourselves to be surprised by what is revealed through these body practices. Rather than thinking we know what our bodies want to say, we cultivate the capacity to truly listen and let our bodies become the teacher.

Meditation: Meal Blessing

> With my whole body I taste these peaches
> I touch them and smell them.
>
> —Wallace Stevens, "A Dish of Peaches in Russia"

One of the ways we can practice this kind of intentional savoring is with our meals. So many of us are disconnected from the true nourishment our food can provide on a physical and spiritual level. We live in a culture of fast food where the motivation is to feed a physical hunger, but when the body is not nourished and the soul is left to hunger, we never feel satisfied.

I invite you to practice mindful eating; by doing so, you can bring the three levels of awareness you have been cultivating.

When you prepare something to eat, ask: Is this nourishing or depleting? Is my food fresh and vibrant or depleted of its nourishment through processing and convenience? Asking these questions is not about guilt or shame with our food choices but about listening deeply to our bodies in order to ask them what will bring the most vibrancy and then choosing from that place of body wisdom.

Before you eat, pause as in the practice of *statio* and breathe. Allow five full breaths to bring yourself fully to this meal, to this moment, and to this act of nourishment. Offer a blessing for this meal. Allow at least one full breath between each mouthful, pausing regularly throughout the meal.

Allow yourself to savor the meal fully with each bite. Take in the taste, texture, aroma, and beauty of the food. Light a candle and play some quiet music if that would support your experience. Sometimes my senses can be overstimulated by too many sensory things happening, so honor what you need to fully enjoy and enter into this meal as a time of encounter with the One who nourishes. If eating the entire meal mindfully feels overwhelming or too much to begin with, consider choosing one part of the meal on your plate to eat consciously with mindful bites. You can slowly work toward the whole meal, but be gentle with yourself.

I invite you to consider writing your own meal blessing to read before you sit down to eat each day. See if you might make one meal each day slow and spacious and reverential. You may already have meal blessings you use. This is an opportunity to revisit those and to be intentional about the kind of awareness you want to cultivate around food for yourself.

The traditional Catholic meal blessing is as follows:

> Bless us,
> O Lord,
> and these your gifts,
> which we are about to receive
> from your bounty.

Through Christ our Lord.
Amen.

Responses to the Meal Blessing

Jesus, made known in the breaking of the
    bread
stay with us here and bless this food.
Stop us
Replenish us
Send us on our way
Fed with your strength, your generosity,
    and your hope.
Amen.

—Bridget McManus

A Blessing for Food

I speak blessing on this food.
I speak blessing on these creatures,
who gave their lives that I might live.
I speak blessing on my body and on my
    soul.
May both be nourished by this eucharist.
I speak blessing on the bodies and souls
    and hands
of those who brought this food to my
    table.
I speak blessing to you, holy abundant
    Mothergod
who speaks nothing but blessing to me.

—Deborah Delano

In this brief moment

I watch your hands
break the bread

And I am thankful

In this brief moment

I am one with the
whole world

Plenty . . . or empty

In this brief moment
Mind and body savour
life
In all its fullness

—Caroline Moore

Write your own version, one that supports you in remembering the
goodness of nourishing your body in order to bring it vitality and aliveness. Listen to the words that would honor your own being.

If you are feeling inspired by this idea of blessing, consider also writing a blessing before bathing, and let your bath or shower become a time
of savoring and presence to the goodness of creation. Part of the Celtic
tradition is to bless every moment and threshold of the day to make
ourselves more fully aware of the Divine dancing with us. Here is one
example of a blessing for your body at this time of day:

Bath/Shower Blessing

Blessed are you, O God, for the gift of
water, water warm and hot.
Blessed are you, O God, for the gift of
lavender, to soothe and balance.
Blessed are you, O God, for the gift of
healing, in making the rough places
smooth.

—Leanne Shawler

Creative Exploration: Creating an Altar and Ritual for the Senses

I invite you again into an expressive arts journey to explore what is emerging for you in these reflections. Begin by creating a simple ritual for your senses. Think about the six senses, and consider putting together a small home altar to remind you of the gifts of the senses as portals to the Divine.

Whether you have a home altar already (or perhaps even several) or have never given it a thought, I invite you to create a sacred space at home dedicated to awakening your senses. Let this be a special place in a private corner, a windowsill, or a decorative table where you will gather symbols for each of the five senses as reminders and talismans for the journey ahead. You will also create a simple ritual to accompany your altar.

For the visual sense, include an icon or a piece of art or photograph you have that evokes a sense of the sacred for you. Or include a mirror so you can see the divine spark in you. For the sense of hearing, include a chime or one of your favorite CDs, or perhaps your altar is by a window that can be opened onto the sounds of birdsong. For the sense of taste, include a piece of deep, dark chocolate, the kind that you really only want to eat one or two pieces of and savor slowly, or a small jar of honey (locally made if possible). For smell, include some massage oil scented with essential oils as a fragrant reminder of God's presence in earthy things or a small vase of fresh flowers. Your oil could serve a dual purpose for touch, as the act of anointing awakens us to the healing act of touch. Or you could have a soft blanket or shawl that you wrap yourself in. Include some symbols from nature such as stones or twigs that you can engage with in a tactile way. For your sixth sense, include a journal, a place to write down whatever rises up in your intuition when you sit down to listen.

Let this be a place you return to each day, even if only for a few minutes. Spend time in this space breathing deeply, welcoming in the greening power of God, and savoring life.

For the ritual, begin by anointing yourself with oil. Maybe you say a simple blessing that each of your senses will be a conduit to the sacred that day. Bless your eyes, ears, nose, mouth, and skin. Receive the gifts of the oil through scent and touch.

Bow to the image on your altar that brings you connection to the Divine through sight.

Play a favorite piece of music, and let yourself enter into its rhythms with your body. If you notice resistance, be with that. Dance with the resistance. You don't have to feel a particular way in this experience. See if you can welcome in where you are physically and emotionally.

When you come to a place of completion with the dance, bow again in reverence to God, who dwells within your own holy body.

Take a piece of the chocolate (or other special treat) and eat it slowly, again as an act of savoring and awakening the senses.

Sit for a few moments in silence, wrapped in a soft blanket or shawl, savoring what is happening within you.

What if you moved through this ritual of the senses each day? If you feel silly or extravagant or if other internal judgments arise, see if you can make space for these without shame or the need to change your commitment. Remember that paying attention to the process and what is unfolding for you is the most valuable element in this work.

Reflection on Her Altar

Fragrant rose buds,
sweet dried cranberries,
a shell with the sound of the ocean,
a fuzzy silk tree seed head,
a crystal,
remind me of the variety and intensity of
    my senses.

—Claire Donovan

Movement Exploration

Yin Yoga: Supported Bridge

Supported bridge

Bridge pose in yin yoga is very similar to regular bridge pose except that you use a block or bolster under your lower spine at your sacrum to support your upward arch and then relax into the stretch, breathing and softening.

The sacrum is the large bone at the base of your spine. If you do not have a block or bolster, roll up a towel tightly to create some lift instead.

Lying down on the floor or a mat, place your feet flat on the floor and close to your buttocks. Pushing down through your feet, lift up your lower back and place the block, bolster, or rolled towel or blanket underneath. It may take a moment or two to find the right position so you feel at ease. Remember you should never feel any pain, so be sure to come out of the pose if you do.

Once you find the right position for your body, take several deep breaths here. If you find you can't breathe deeply at any time, back off from the pose. After you've found the right position for your body, soften into the experience. Let your senses be heightened during this time, especially your kinesthetic sense. Notice what you feel physically and where in your body the feeling is located. Every time a new sensation arises, bring your breath to that place and hold an open and loving curiosity and attention.

Once your time is done, very gently ease off the block, bolster, towel, or blanket, and then hug your knees into your chest, rocking back and forth on your spine. Yin requires us to be very gentle in our transitions.

Shape and Stillness

Another of my favorite forms from InterPlay is called Shape and Stillness. For this practice, find a piece of slow-paced music, and begin the dance by coming into a standing position, feet hip-width apart, arms extended downward, and head tall. Connect with the rhythm of your natural breath, following its rise and fall. Then deepen your breath, bringing it down into your diaphragm so that your belly expands. Rest into the stillness for a few moments.

As you tune into your body, begin to allow yourself to move into a shape and then hold it. This can be any shape that feels good to explore. You might think of this as making up your own yoga pose, but you do not need to have any intention of stretching. Your only focus is moving into a shape, any shape at all, and then holding it for a few breaths, savoring the experience fully with your senses. Pausing allows you in this moment to fully experience what is happening. Then as you feel led, transition gently into another shape and hold it again in stillness for several breaths. Notice if thoughts arise about what shapes your body should make, and let those go, only following the body's impulses. Play with moving quickly between shapes so as to bypass the mind. Move slowly again. In this way, move gently from shape to shape, allowing pauses in between to breathe deeply, to savor, and to explore what sensations arise in your body in response to your movement.

As you pause in each shape your body moves into, see if you can fully inhabit that form. Notice what your senses reveal to you in this moment. What do you see, smell, taste, feel, hear, and discover? Let this be an exploration of following your curiosity. What does this particular shape feel like in your body? Does it bring your senses alive or not? Notice without judgment. Keep returning to your breath.

As the music comes to the end, find a final gesture that feels like a satisfying conclusion to this embodied prayer. Rest into the silence for several breaths.

Follow with some journal writing to explore what you noticed and discovered.

Reflection Questions

- Where have you traveled through the thresholds of your senses?
- What were the moments that reminded you of the sacramentality of your own flesh?
- What are you discovering through the slow ripening of your awareness?

Closing Blessing

Body Psalm for Savoring

Enough is Enough
it is way too much doing, thinking, producing
and thinking about doing more when it may
be time to do less

be less, lessen and here is the lesson
You have already produced more beauty, generosity and
work through one creative endeavor or another for several lifetimes
not to mention children you have raised, parents you have attended to
gardens you have planted, literally and metaphorically
and brought more people, projects and passions to ripening
than can be counted
you are past counting
and now it is time to be countless
and perhaps be a countess
Relax into a place of knowing
that you have already
done enough
and now is the time to
S A V O R
Savor all the ways you have worked with your whole heart
and loved with your whole heart:
mothers, fathers, siblings, friends, children, lovers, spouses and
even those who have left your life through natural or unnatural causes
Accept all your luxurious beauty of soulfulness that has wrapped
around those you hold in your heart
and all the efforts you have made to follow meaning
in the world through work, words, worries and wantings
Vibrate with all that is going through you—
the rise and fall of internal waves
crashes of questions
hormonal fluctuations in a sea of ripenings
Own both your shortcomings and accomplishments
which means to name and rename what you truly
have done, don't dismiss it in light of living into the unknown
Others own all your wonder, it is time for you to own it too
Relinquish the need to be superwoman or superman
have a funeral for doing too much
and celebrate not doing in some way
Enjoy being and know you are being formed into a wise one
You are being called to drink from the cup of serene

Each gesture is an act of love
a counteraction to a world of overdoing
an addiction to doing one more thing
when all along
the love in your eyes
the way you behold
who and what you love
is the fragrance of
the One who gave
the beautiful scent
of you.

—Celeste Snowber

Chapter 4

Feelings and Desire:
The Ocean of Emotion

So don't be frightened, dear friend, if a sadness confronts you larger than any you have ever known, casting its shadow over all you do. You must think that something is happening within you, and remember that life has not forgotten you; It holds you in its hand and will not let you fall. Why would you want to exclude from your life any uneasiness, any pain, any depression, since you don't know what work they are accomplishing within you?

—Rainer Maria Rilke,
Letters to a Young Poet

In this chapter we dive into the realm of feelings and desires as a way of growing in intimacy with our bodies. If breath is the gateway into our bodies and the senses are the way we experience the world around us, feelings are the language of the body's experience, how the body speaks and reveals her wisdom. Through observation we can open ourselves to allowing the fullness of our emotions to move through us.

Feelings are the bridge between mind and body, and they become an embodied language of our experience. Emotions can be described as energy in motion, and when we block off the experience, that energy becomes trapped in our bodies.

We are often taught to fear certain feelings and shut ourselves off from them. Western culture, especially in the United States, is one of perpetual optimism. We are encouraged never to be with our grief but to cheer up and move on. Rather than following Rilke's wise advice, we miss the opportunity to come to know what work these feelings are crafting within us.

Over time we may begin to discover that feelings often come in waves. If we stop resisting the intensity of our experience and instead soften into it, we can allow it to move through us. It no longer becomes stuck but is allowed to have its movement, and so the intensity rises and then naturally recedes, often leaving a sense of deeper calm in its wake.

Deepest Desires

> Uncover what you long for and you will discover who you are.
>
> —Phil Cousineau, *The Art of Pilgrimage*

One of the great elements of wisdom we have inherited from St. Ignatius of Loyola, that sixteenth-century Spanish soldier-turned-mystic, is the fundamental belief that our deepest desires have been planted there by God. Sounds simple, right? We just follow those deep desires, and we follow our call in the world. Except that, as human beings, we seem to have all kinds of ingrained mechanisms to get in our own way.

There are those feelings we want so much to resist, creating all kinds of stuckness inside of ourselves, a dam of emotions waiting to break free.

There are the messages that our desires are not to be trusted. Isn't this what the story of Eve, at least in its traditional interpretations, is trying to tell us? Eve followed her desires, and the whole world was exiled from Paradise. Do we all carry some version of that message deep within? Do we hold some fundamental mistrust that our own desires can be good and nourishing, bringing us to the threshold of the sacred and carrying possibility of opening to places long shut down?

Part of what we need to do is distinguish between desire and craving or compulsion. Richard Rohr describes the gap between the two as the difference between being driven and being drawn.[1] Being driven is the force of ego imposing its will on others; being drawn is the soul yielding to its call in the world.

Desire is a longing within us for what brings us to life, and in the process of giving space for that aliveness, we connect to our calling in the world and who God created us to be.

But we seem to desire so many things. When I feel tired, lonely, or overwhelmed, food becomes such a desirable companion. But it has a different quality from the things I desire, such as serving my community with my gifts of writing and teaching, where I feel myself extending my hands in openness, ready to receive as well as give. The desires I feel out of a sense of need or lack are really the shadow side: they are compulsions. There is a tightness to these, a grasping.

Hildegard of Bingen described the vices as the twisted form of the virtues so that the more we come to know our own "vices," which we might call compulsions or stuck places, the more we can come to know the other side of those that is our heart's deep desire, our longing to respond to the world from love. It comes down to the distinction between ego cravings and soul desires.

The desire for food as filling a void and the sense of grasping that can accompany it, when not out of a physical hunger, is very different than the desire to savor a beautifully prepared meal. When I crave, I always want to have more as I fear there will never be enough. Craving and compulsion are motivated by a sense of scarcity and the desire for immediate gratification.

My soul desires are not motivated by scarcity. The soul holds expectations loosely and is not attached to the outcome. The soul takes her time, embraces the slow ripening of things, and savors what is to be learned from the process. I can take a deep breath and feel a sense of spaciousness around my soul desires.

We tune into the ego cravings and compulsions usually through our thoughts; they are the loudspeaker offering a never-ending narrative of what we want, what we fear, and what we think isn't good enough. We hear a lot of shoulds and musts. The ego thrives on anxiety, which traps us inside our heads with this cavalcade of thoughts and judgments.

We tune into the soul's desires through the body; breath helps us to slow down and receive this moment. We pay attention to what makes our bodies feel more alive. The senses help us attune ourselves to what is happening in our bodies. We discover the soul's desires by paying attention to the synchronicities of life and intuitive, embodied knowing. The soul thrives on slowness, spaciousness, and stillness.

Sexuality and the Erotic Impulse

Rilke said that God speaks in our longings. As I mentioned in chapter 3, the medieval monks were fascinated by the Song of Songs as a poem of heightened desire. It was read as an allegory of Israel's love for God or the monk's love for Christ. This ancient erotic love poem teaches us how to follow those desires that lead to deeper love. The sexual excitement described explicitly in the Song is a symbol for spiritual anticipation. And at the same time, by allowing the erotic to be a metaphor for the holy, the Song sanctifies the beauty of this kind of love.

We are continually bombarded with suggestions of what we should desire, generally things that cost us money and keep us feeling inadequate. And when we voice our desires, we are deemed suspect or sinful. No wonder we feel conflicted about claiming what our hearts most deeply long for.

Sexuality and the erotic are fundamental urges we have as human beings to move us beyond our solipsistic, preoccupied selves into a world of community and connection. Sexuality is about more than sex in the physical sense—although making love is one of the great sensual gifts we have been created for, and the extraordinary pleasure it brings to our bodies surely points to a God who finds this kind of erotic delight a beautiful thing. The act of lovemaking can be a place of profound ecstasy, of moving beyond your own perceived boundaries into vulnerable and intimate connection with another in the context of deep trust and commitment.

What if our call is to make love to life itself, whether or not we express it in a physically intimate way with another person? What if this sexual desire were about tapping into a source of energy that awakens us to our deepest longing for connection?

Sexuality is what draws us beyond our own boundaries into the service, intimacy, and vulnerability of human relationships. Our deepest desires thrust us into these places of tenderness that come with meaningful human connection. Our deep desires of the heart are about bringing our gifts into the world to make a difference. We are called to move beyond the sphere of self-concern into a dance of mutuality with others where we are invited to believe that our existence makes a difference in the human-animal-nature community.

To go back to the language of the desert monks, when our desires have become distorted and under the control of the ego and the mind's thoughts, we find ourselves craving and compulsive; we grasp and feel as though there is never enough food, enough money, and enough love. We become enslaved by these desires in their shadow forms.

Spirituality is always a movement toward freedom. As we become clearer about our places of wounding, we gain freedom because we don't have to live from these unconscious impulses.

Gregory Mayers describes it this way in *Listen to the Desert*: "The task, then, is not to avoid what makes me tearful, ashamed, or angry, or to entertain it, or even to act the emotions out. Both efforts, repression and expression, can lead to an emotional trap that bogs one down in the anger, shame, or fear. The task is to attend to them, acknowledge them, give them their full and rightful place in the community of the self."[2] He later goes on to write:

> These two emotions, shame and fear, shield us from our own tumultuous unconscious. Everyone learns early in life that shame guards what we believe is unacceptable about ourselves. But if we are to become whole, sooner or later we must summon the courage to enter the pit of shame in our backyard and deal with it, engage the demons, and pull up the hidden things about our self buried there. These discarded and unknown fragments

of our self will serve us and others well when they are cleaned of our shame, redeemed from the well of our own dark side, and seen for what they are. They too have a place in us. We are incomplete and fractured until we welcome and embrace them in friendship and love.[3]

When our desire and compulsions are healed and integrated, they become the source for tremendous energy for good in the world and our ability to be a healing presence to others. But first we must reclaim all that has been discarded, all that has been denied.

The body has so much to teach us about the goodness of desire. When we slow down and savor, we thwart the compulsion to consume things, to move too quickly through life. Sexuality calls us to reclaim that which has been rejected and enter into intimate relationship with it.

Underneath the armor of our bodies against feeling our emotions is a deep well of desire. It may feel at first like grief when we let ourselves sink down into it—grief over the missed opportunities or time spent doing things that have depleted us. Stay with the grief; let it move through you in waves until you reach the place of stillness underneath, the place where you can hear your desires shimmering forth. The grief must have room to flow through, or it will remain a wall of resistance keeping you from accessing those deeper desires more freely.

Ally on the Journey: Eve

> When Eve bit into the apple, she gave us the world as we know the world—beautiful, flawed, dangerous, full of being. . . . All we know of heaven we know from Eve, who gave us earth, a serviceable blueprint: Without Eve there would be no utopias, no imaginable reason to find and to create transcendence, to ascend toward the light. Eve's legacy to us is the imperative to desire.
>
> —Barbara Grizzuti Harrison,
> "A Meditation on Eve," in *Out of the Garden*

Joining our circle of allies and support comes Eve, the mythical first woman. Much of my appreciation of Eve's gifts for us comes from the writing of theologian and colleague Ronna Detrick. Detrick does such beautiful work in helping us to reclaim Eve's desires in that ancient narrative as good, desires that led her into a world of freedom and beauty. Detrick breaks open Eve's story as a story for all women who want to explore the places where they have been told their desires are corrupt or destructive.[4]

As Harrison's quotation suggests, we can learn much about desire from Eve and how to appreciate a world so full of terrible suffering but also beauty and wondrous moments. Eve, while much maligned in more traditional theological interpretations, is the mythical first woman from whom our own stories unfold.

Invite Eve to become a wise guide for discerning the desires that bring you nourishment and life and those that arise from compulsion and grasping.

Practice: Radical Hospitality and Welcome

St. Benedict wrote in his Rule, "All guests who present themselves are to be welcomed as Christ, for he himself will say: *I was a stranger and you welcomed me.*" The core of this idea was that everyone who comes to the door of the monastery and, by extension, the door to our lives—the poor, the traveler, or the curious, and those of a different religion, social class, or education—should be welcomed in, not just as an honored guest but also as a window onto the sacred presence. For Benedict, our encounters with the stranger—the unknown, the unexpected, and the foreign elements that spark our fear—are precisely where we are most likely to encounter God. This is a practice of outer hospitality.

The concept of *inner* hospitality is to open our inner selves to all of the elements about us that we fear and reject—the painful and dark feelings, our shadow side, or the things we do and long for that we don't want anyone else to know about. If we embrace Benedict's wisdom for our deepest selves, inner hospitality might be seen as hospitality that proceeds from the very core or root of who we are and an invitation to extend a welcome to the stranger who dwells inside of us.

We are each made up of multiple inner characters and voices; some of them get invited to our inner table, while others stand out in the rain waiting to be let in to feast and share their wisdom with us. In this practice, I invite you to befriend any feelings that you have held at arm's length or suppressed. Often this is grief or anger that has not been allowed expression.

How do you welcome in the range of your feelings without being swept away by them? One way to do this is by cultivating your inner witness and connecting regularly with your calm, nonanxious, compassionate core self. Meditation practice can nurture our ability to sit and observe the rise and fall of our inner lives without resisting or seizing any particular moment. When we offer ourselves the space to simply be with whatever is happening inside us without judgment, we begin to see that each of those feelings passes with time. When you notice yourself resisting an inner voice or shutting your inner door on it, take some time to intentionally invite this voice inside to the table. Ask it what it has come to tell you. Listen past the first layer, which may sound ugly or painful, and tend to the deeper layers underneath. This takes time, much like growing in intimacy with a friend. Our rejected selves will need some coaxing.

When we choose to receive guests as a window into the sacred presence, we choose to live and relate from a more intentional and reverential place. When we engage in a dynamic encounter with what we are fearful of, it relinquishes its power on us, and new wisdom and energy are released. It is in this place of hospitality to the unknown where we encounter God.

In meditation we cultivate our ability to be completely present to the rise and fall of our emotions not by becoming detached or disassociated from them but by fully experiencing them without feeling carried away by their power. The art-making process offers the same invitation: to be present to what is happening within us, to notice the fears and judgments rising and falling. The witness is the compassionate and curious part of ourselves that is able to look with love and tenderness on this pattern rising up in us and to extend a sense of curiosity.

Meditation: Welcoming Prayer

The Welcoming Prayer is a practice of intentionally inviting your feelings into your experience. This practice was originally developed by Contemplative Outreach's late master teacher Mary Mrozowski. It is based largely on the teaching and wisdom of Fr. Thomas Keating and an eighteenth-century work titled *Abandonment to Divine Providence* by Jean Pierre de Caussade.

There are three main movements to the process of the Welcoming Prayer:

1. Focus and sink in
2. Welcome
3. Let go

You begin the practice by allowing some time to move your focus and attention to your body. Allow some time to breathe and connect with what you are experiencing. Notice both physical pain and emotions. Bring your full awareness to whatever the experience is without trying to change it. Notice how you experience this in your body. If you feel sad, how is that manifested in your body? Don't try to change anything. Just stay present. Focusing doesn't mean psychoanalyzing. This is not about trying to discover why you feel the way you do or justifying your feelings.

This first step is the key to the whole practice. By becoming physically aware of emotion as sensation in your body, you can stay in the present and welcome the feeling, which is the second movement.

When you feel fully immersed in the feeling or experience, you begin to practice this inner hospitality and say very gently, "Welcome, anger," or "Welcome, sorrow, welcome." If you aren't sure which emotion is arising, just say, "Welcome," without naming it. The goal of this practice is not to get rid of the experience you're having but not to let it take your awareness from being fully present to yourself and this moment.

What often happens when we experience something we consider negative is that we begin to immediately resist the feeling. We may distract ourselves or try to figure out what is wrong, but both of these responses simply move us further away from an experience of this moment in time. By embracing the thing you once defended yourself against or ran from, you actually open yourself to hear the wisdom it might have to offer, to reveal what it is trying to say to you.

When we allow ourselves to be fully present to our experience, a remarkable thing happens: we find the courage and strength to stay with the moment. The inner witness is rooted in the divine presence within and is able to be fully present to whatever is happening from a place of calm and compassion. Your inner witness allows you to have the strength to stay with your experience no matter its physical or psychological impact.

In this practice we stay present and welcome feelings in, but we don't identify with them. We come to recognize that this experience doesn't define the whole of who we are. We are not made up entirely of our grief just as we are not fully defined by our joy.

This act of welcome doesn't ask you to condone the situation that caused the physical or emotional pain. Surrender isn't about accepting illness, rejection, or pain inflicted by another as somehow just the way life is. Rather, you are welcoming in the feelings the experience evokes for you and letting them have some space within. This is surrender as an inner attitude rather than an outer practice. Sometimes the events of our lives demand our resistance; sometimes we are called to say no. But the feelings we experience need room within our bodies.

If you start to feel overwhelmed in any way, return to your breath as an anchor, and let go of the process for the time being, returning only when you feel ready again.

The third step is letting go, but the temptation might be to move here too quickly. The real work of the Welcoming Prayer is in those first two steps, staying with the experience as long as it needs and welcoming it in until the wall of resistance begins to come down on its own. When you feel this inner fighting of the experience dissolve, then you can begin to practice letting go. This practice of letting go is just for now because as human beings we will continue to encounter the difficult emotions. This is not a final, forever renunciation of your anger or fear; it's simply a way of gently waving farewell as the emotion starts to recede. If you experience resistance to the letting go, don't pretend; simply accept where you are right now and bring some compassion to yourself. To let go you might say something simple, such as, "I let go of my anger and give it over to God."

Take some time right now; begin with a few minutes to focus on what you are experiencing without changing it. Once you name the feeling, welcome it in. Stay with it as long as you need to, seeing if you can simply accept this as the truth of your life in this moment. When you feel a bit of release around your resistance, practice letting go, not holding on to whatever this was, knowing that each moment brings its own grace and truth.

Responses to the Welcoming Prayer

Welcome, welcome, welcome
Fear of Future.
Sit down with me and have some coffee.
Milk? Sugar? Are you comfortable?
Good.
But I am not comfortable with you.
You show up at my home at the most
    inopportune times, lurk around
    corners, get in
my way in my kitchen, while I entertain
    friends, even as I lie in my bed!
In all this time I have never thought to
    ask you
What brings you to my door?
How did you get my address in the first
    place?
Now I am asking. We are going to have
    some talks
You and I

And you are going to give up some of
    your secrets to me.
And I believe
In time,
The One Who Sees Me
Will transform you and give you a new
    name.
No longer Fear of the Future
Or Fear of Old Age
Or Fear of Dying Alone and Homeless.
You shall be called
Confidence in the One Who Sees Me.
Until then, let's keep having these chats.
I believe we both have much to learn
    from one another.

—Debra Strahan

Welcome? Who thought I would say
    welcome to my pulsating, stabbing,
    ever-permeating pain and my bone-
    weary, weighted fatigue? It feels
    wrong. My resistance is high so I
    speak the words aloud

Welcome pain.
Welcome weariness.
Welcome fear.
You do not define me, but you are part of
    me.

—Lisa Murray

welcoming in my fear
contrary to my usual experience

of trying to analyze it,
deny it
or change myself
into being a stronger person

my chest
the upper body under my chin
was slightly constricted
welcome in fear,
welcome, welcome, welcome
you have a place of rest here
you can stay as long as you need to
you are a part of my landscape
I welcome you

no need to run away
strength moves in
lungs are expanding
the chest space is opening
thank you for being here
I can now let you go!

—Camilla Caughlin

Creative Exploration: Collage of Desire

For this art exploration you will need a magazine with images, a piece of paper (I would keep this limited to an eight and a half by eleven at most and consider cutting it into a square shape), scissors, and a glue stick. For the magazine images, you are welcome to use catalogs, but be mindful of those with unhealthy body images; since these unhealthy body images can also be found in magazine advertising, finding magazines not marketed solely to women can be helpful. *National Geographic* works very well as the paper is good quality and old copies are often available in used bookstores. Used art books are another good option, and tearing out pages can be very satisfying.

Collage is a powerful medium because it makes visual art very accessible to people who get stuck over a fear they can't draw. It is also powerful on a metaphorical level because it brings together disparate images into an expression of wholeness.

Gently hold the question "What is my heart's deep desire?" as you begin. You are not trying to answer this question so much as plant a seed of awareness.

As you look through images, I always recommend allowing the images to choose you; pay attention both to images that create a sense of resonance—ones you are really drawn to and that spark a sense of joy or aliveness in you—and to images that create a sense of dissonance— aversion or resistance—in you. These strong energetic responses provide clues to things within you that want expression. The dissonance is often revelatory of shadow material that wants illumination and can also free us up to follow our deep desires. Again, while you are in the process, let go of figuring out why certain images call to or repel you; simply include them in your collage and surrender the need to know.

When completed, rest for a few moments with your breath and notice how your body feels. Then allow some time for writing and reflection. Rather than analyzing the images, speak from their voices. A helpful tool is to select one image, write "I am" on the image, and then speak from that voice. See what each one has to say to you and then enter them in conversation with one another.

Response to the Collage

Field of Flowers

Let me surround you with beauty, colour,
    vitality and life;
Let me surprise you with joy every
    morning when you open your blinds;

Let me tickle your toes and caress your
    summer legs as you walk through
    me;
Let me be a habitat for all manner of bee,
    fly and earthworm;
Let me spread this joy to all who share
    your home and life.

                                  —Judith King

Movement Exploration

Yin Yoga: Frog

Frog can be one of the more intense yoga poses. It is a powerful hip opener. Look up the video instructions for the pose online. You may want to have a block or bolster to put underneath you for extra support if the stretch becomes too intense.

In frog you begin by coming onto your hands and knees. Then lower your arms down onto your elbows so you are resting on your forearms for support. When you are comfortable in this position, begin to spread your legs outward, keeping the bend in the knee. If the stretch is too intense, place a bolster underneath you for support. Relax your head down. You shouldn't have any tension in your neck.

Once in the pose, allow a few slow, deep breaths. Breathing helps us to stay present in the midst of the intensity. Notice physical sensations, and create space for those to unfold. You don't have to change anything in your inner experience other than bringing a compassionate awareness to what is unfolding. Feelings often rise up when we place our bodies in these different postures. This is a perfect time to practice allowing those feelings to move through us without resistance or direction.

We can give ourselves the gift of these three to five minutes of simply breathing and paying attention to how our feelings want to rise and fall. At the end of the pose, release your arms and legs from supporting you, and let yourself relax on the floor with your head turned to one side and your cheek resting on your mat. Allow a few moments to bask in the experience of release and to notice what feelings arise now.

Dancing the Waves of Emotion

Play a piece of music you love. As always, begin with breathing and bringing your awareness into your body. If grief arises, let this be a dance with grief. If anger stirs, let this be a dance with anger. Allow yourself to have whatever experience you are having without judgment, only gentle curiosity. Let the dance be a time of allowing your body to move as it longs to; listen to the desires of your body in the dance.

I try and dance each day to at least one song after my yoga practice. Dance and anything that moves energy can be very good after a yin practice because yin works to open our energy channels, so the dance helps get the energy flowing through. Often I begin to weep as the music starts and my body moves; most of the time I have no idea why. But I have learned to trust this wave of emotion, and I surrender to it. It feels incredibly good to allow myself space to cry, to let the tears fall, even if I do not know where they come from. I do not have to figure out why I am feeling a particular way. Often our attempt to figure a feeling out is an attempt to control it, as if we need to justify why we are having the experience we are having.

Imagine resting into your heart center and letting the desires of your heart have a dance this day. How does your body want to move in response? Listen in. You don't have to figure out what this means; you can simply have the experience.

Reflection Questions

- What stirs in your heart as we move through these invitations to experience your feelings and name your desires?
- What has been your own relationship to sexuality? Which stories have you told yourself that have hindered you, and which have freed you?
- What are you noticing as you deepen into the practice of movement?

Closing Blessing

Body Psalm for Celebrating Your Sexuality

You are a juicy orange
papaya split in half
mango on fire
wrapped in the luxuriousness
of a wo/man with flesh and heart
tender and strong
waiting to be honored
by your own deep soul.
It is the life-force
energy of life itself—eros of day
the pulsing blood of vibrancy
running through your cells
enlivening the fabric of your being
which is the ground of your sexuality.
Here is the template
to embrace your own temple
the widening one of love

living in your solar plexus
connected to the creation of the universe.
It is not the breasts, chests,
vagina, penis that holds your sexuality
but what rises within you
and works in harmony
with your dear body
You can so easily confuse the
outer as the source of beauty
and the entrance to sexual aliveness
when you are being awakened
from a much deeper center
and your sensual knowledge
calls you home
to the delight of presence
the wind on your chest
the expanse in your back
the thrill of naked feet in sand
places of release
invite you to sense from the inside out
now is the time
to love back your body to itself
live in a state of open
where the cords of fire
will rip through your body
and you will know
the deep gift of your own vitality
feeding the heart of sexuality
where all of life is a bedroom
to be awake to each moment
loving each breath
in this place is an ancient shrine
located deep within your own crevices
calling you forth to your own juice
the desire is already within you

it only needs to be honored
for its pure nature
it is what calls you to the divine
to yourself and to the other
and it is not your hips or pelvis
which is sexy, but how you let
the energy of life soar and dance
through your pelvis to say yes
to its own truth
here is your ground
here is your flight.

—Celeste Snowber

Chapter 5

Thoughts:
The Inner Witness

Observance of the soul can be deceptively simple. You take back what has been disowned. You work with what is, rather than with what you wish were there.

—Thomas Moore, *Care of the Soul*

We each have within us a wise, compassionate, calm, and curious part of ourselves that we might call the inner witness. Here dwells the spark of the divine, the place where we can touch a deep inner stillness that the desert monks called *hesychia*. Thomas Merton described it as the True Self.[1] We are able to cultivate and nurture this part of ourselves through contemplative practices that heighten our capacity for presence to each moment. We develop an inner freedom and begin to discover something of the foundation of who we are that endures despite the constantly shifting tides around us.

In the Benedictine monastic tradition, hospitality is a fundamental value. In St. Benedict's Rule he writes, "Let everyone that comes be received as Christ." The invitation is to see every person who arrives at the door (both literal and metaphorical) as bearing a face of God, even the person who annoys or irritates us and the person who makes us feel uncomfortable. Welcome them in especially, says Benedict, because they will reveal God in ways you do not expect.

This extension of hospitality is both an external and internal process. We can extend hospitality to ourselves as well. Chelsea Wakefield, a therapist and dreamworker in North Carolina, uses the metaphor of the inner round table.[2] She suggests we each contain a multiplicity of selves—different parts and voices—and we might imagine the round table they gather around as the Self, our core that is able to observe the other parts of ourselves in a compassionate way. The Self is the part of ourselves that the mystics describe as dwelling in God.

In any given moment, we have a variety of inner selves or voices that clamor for our attention. We practice meditation or art-making, in part, to become present to those voices. Rather than resisting the voices we dislike, our invitation is to welcome them in and open up a hospitable space within ourselves. We often spend so much energy resisting these unwelcome parts of our inner world. When we are in a place of balance, the Self is the center of our focus, and each voice has its place around the table in conversation with the others. When our energy becomes obsessed with a particular identity or voice, the dynamic shifts away from centering in the True Self.

The Self is the calm, nonanxious core we all possess, which is able to witness this internal process. In meditation we cultivate our ability to be completely present to the rise and fall of our emotions not by becoming detached or disassociated from them but by fully experiencing them without feeling carried away by their power. Both dance and art-making offer the same invitation: to be present to what is happening within us, to notice the fears and judgments rising and falling. The witness is able to look with love and tenderness on this pattern rising up in us and extend a sense of curiosity. We might then ask ourselves, "Why is this coming up right now in this time and place? What does this wave of feeling have to say to me of importance about myself and God? Where else in my life do I experience these voices?" Witnessing is not about fixing something; witnessing is about entering into a relationship with what *is* and discovering the grace and gifts hidden there.

The more we practice accessing our witness, the stronger it becomes for us. The witness is what helps us to observe our patterns and begin to make new choices.

Mindfulness

> As for the body, it is solid, it is strong and curious and
> full of detail. . . . It is the only vessel in the world that
> can hold, in a mix of power and sweetness: words, song,
> gesture, passion, ideas.
>
> —Mary Oliver, *Evidence*

Mindfulness is a word we hear a lot these days. There seems to be no
end of resources offering ways to practice it. Essentially it is a practice of
having a loving awareness of the present moment. To be mindful means
that we bring our witness to work by observing our actions and what is
happening inside of us.

To wash dishes in a mindful way, I will become aware of each moment rather than try to distract myself with television, music, or even
daydreaming. I will feel the warmth of the water and the texture of the
soap. I will feel the sponge in my hand as I scrub it across the plate. I will
simply bring all of my attention to whatever I am doing in the moment.
Mindfulness is the opposite of multitasking, where we do several things
at once and usually none of them well. When we are mindful we have the
opportunity to focus on one thing or task at a time in order to appreciate
the moment.

Similarly I can bring mindfulness to my inner life as well. Perhaps I
am having a conversation with a friend and experience tension because
of some unnamed conflict. I can become aware of how my body feels
and what emotions move through me. I can bring my attention to the
thoughts that are rising up, especially those that seem to be persistent
and repetitive.

In mindfulness I do not judge these things as good or bad; I simply
notice what my reality is or the truth of this moment. Then I can make a
choice to direct my thoughts in a more loving or open way.

Working with Thoughts

> The struggle with the self was hardly simple. It meant
> grappling continuously with those parts of the self the
> monks called the passions, those anomalous, unhealed
> parts of the soul, and the demons who brought them
> into the monks' conscious and unconscious awareness.
>
> —Douglas Christie, *The Blue Sapphire of the Mind*

Our thoughts, often rooted in the ego's perception of things, originate in our minds and can often feel like a tyrannical onslaught. Many of us resist sitting in silence because we are afraid of the inner noise awaiting us.

Sometimes when I walk into the elevator of my building, where there is a full-length mirror along one wall, a negative thought about my body arises before I am even conscious of what is happening. It could be a general weight thought, a body-part thought, or some other form of internal criticism and judgment. Sometimes I find myself leaning into my reflection to scrutinize some aspect of myself before I go face the world outside. I let myself get caught into the drama of this thought and follow its trail of criticism, which might look like an escalating series of self-judgments about how I look or a sometimes even more pernicious form of self-criticism in the form of *What am I thinking? I am an aware and liberated woman; how could I possibly even have these thoughts?* Suddenly I am trapped in a judgment of a different kind. Either way, the nature of thoughts is that they spiral when unobserved, getting us entangled in their web of destructive lies that only serve to diminish us. Working with mindfulness, I can observe this happening and prevent it from controlling me.

In the desert tradition working with mindfulness was called "watchfulness" or *prosoche*. When I'm watchful I allow my inner witness to notice what is happening, name it for what it is, and then say a strong no to the cycle of negative thoughts rising up. Think about how much energy we waste with this internalized criticism and judgment. Think how exhausting this endless self-analysis becomes.

Watchfulness is an empowering practice in which we stay present to our experience and root out those thoughts that are depleting and destructive. These thoughts were often referred to as "demons" in the ancient desert, which indicated a way of understanding the inner and outer forces, temptations, voices, and judgments that lead us away from the heart of God. Demons are those energies that scatter our attention, that disrupt our ability to stay present and centered. The Desert Fathers and Mothers realized early on that their thoughts influenced their actions, so they worked at rooting out and letting go of the thoughts and patterns that undermined their behaviors.

Often the metaphor they used was doing "battle" with thoughts. Battle is an archetypal idea, with the warrior as an ancient expression of the one who goes to battle. Warrior energy is something we all carry within us to varying degrees; it calls us to be fierce protectors of our boundaries. The warrior in each of us is able to say no very clearly to what is not nourishing or life-giving.

The goal wasn't to eradicate these thoughts—this isn't possible as human beings—but to recognize the lifelong journey of staying present and aware. We can approach this with a fierce gentleness.

The Stories We Tell Ourselves

Similar to these patterns of thought that cycle through our minds are stories: persistent thoughts that have coalesced into a narrative. We likely all have stories about something in our life that we repeat to ourselves in subtle ways. Perhaps the story is that "I am not a dancer" or "I am not creative." These stories are rooted in a concrete experience, usually one involving some shame. We get stuck in these stories, limiting our range of possibility.

For years I lived with debilitating chronic illness. I went on disability and wondered often if I would ever be able to financially support myself. I carried a great deal of fear about having enough energy and money. I had a story that I was disabled and unable to work full time.

Thankfully, with the development of better medications and my own growing ability to nourish myself well through a variety of means,

I was able to work more over time. Throughout my doctoral studies I often worked many long hours. However, I dismissed the work because it wasn't a job; it was something I loved. After finishing graduate school I started working part time at a university as an adjunct professor of theology. I also started leading retreats and developing my own work. Yet somehow I still had this story in my mind that I couldn't work full time even though I was, perhaps because I wasn't able to earn a combined full-time income though I was working many jobs.

It was a limiting story because I kept telling myself I couldn't manage in a full-time job. I felt a great deal of fear around my capabilities even though I was working hard and doing well. Finally a trusted friend heard me tell a version of this story and reflected back to me what she saw, which was very different. After hearing from her, I began to change the story.

Moving Out of Our Heads

The mind can be very much an ally in the journey toward releasing these self-destructive thoughts and limiting stories. Mindfulness is a gift of awareness; through attention comes freedom. But sometimes we need to get out of our heads entirely and let our awareness drop down into our bodies. Sometimes we need to go for a walk when we have been thinking and pushing an idea for too long.

I am very much a thinker. I love pondering deep thoughts. I was a philosophy major in college before I went on to study theology. I have also been a writer for as long as I can remember. I love spending long hours immersed in the writing process. I can get lost in my thoughts and sometimes forget I have a body. Because of these tendencies, I have to be especially diligent when I am working on a writing project to make time for stretching, walking, dancing, and swimming so that my awareness might drop out of my head for a while and I can remember other ways of being in the world.

Our bodies offer us a whole other realm of wisdom, which speaks in a different language and offers us possibilities our minds could never have come up with through analysis and reason. One of the great gifts to me in the act of discernment, which is making decisions rooted in a sense of calling through Spirit, is to recognize how I can't think my way through life decisions. Body sensations, nudges, intuition, and felt senses all offer me valuable information as well.

Ally on the Journey: Amma Syncletica

> Amma Syncletica said, "There are many who live in the mountains and behave as if they were in town, and they are wasting their time. It is possible to be a solitary in one's mind while living in a crowd, and it is possible for one who is a solitary to live in the crowd of his own thoughts."
>
> —Benedicta Ward, *The Sayings of the Desert Fathers*

Our growing circle of allies for this journey toward embodiment now includes Amma Syncletica, one of the early women who went out into the desert of Egypt and Syria to find a different way of life in intimacy with God. Born into a wealthy family in Alexandria in the third century, a community grew around her. She is one of the best known Desert Mothers, and much of her teaching centers around working with thoughts.

She saw no distinction between monks who lived in the desert and monks who lived in the city—the spiritual call for both was the same. She felt that too many people were dwelling in the desert but still acting as though they lived in the city. Despite being in a place of silence and solitude, they continued to carry on with conversation and interaction that distracted them from prayer.

We may find ourselves fantasizing that if we could only move away to a monastery we would meditate perfectly or find wholeness more easily. These are stories that do not serve us. As Amma Syncletica wisely indicates, we can pursue the spiritual life wherever we are. It is our internal disposition, not external circumstances, that is important.

Invite her in to support you as you begin to notice the thoughts that tear you down, and begin to release them.

Practice: Watchfulness and Paying Attention

The Greek word *nepsis* means "watchfulness." It refers to a kind of calm vigilance in daily life, staying attentive to and aware of the inner movements of the heart, watching one's thoughts, and noticing the patterns that arise. It is our inner witness that holds this space and awareness. This inner attention, conducted with compassion, is the grace of the desert way:

> Attention is a skill we can develop and a gift we can receive that unifies the Absolute and everyday life. As a skill it means waking up to whatever flows across the field of attention, whether that is inner or outer experiences, thoughts, feelings, or perceptions. It means not picking and choosing what rises to awareness, and not hanging on to what falls away. It means not being disturbed by the content of attention, *not being obsessed with it, not being compulsive about being attentive.*[3]

The Desert Fathers and Mothers invite us to practice this kind of interior watchfulness where we witness what happens inside our minds and hearts with compassion and commitment but without obsession and compulsion. This continual attentiveness is not like being monitored. Think of it as a loving act of reverence. When we pay attention to what is happening in our inner life, we have the opportunity to notice our own patterns and habits of thought. When the self-criticism and negative stories arise, we can gently pause the narrative in our minds and direct them another way.

Work with consciously changing distorted thoughts that tear you down. Invite in a loving awareness and willingness to meet yourself with great compassion.

Meditation: Remember That You Will One Day Die

We live in a culture very disconnected from the reality of death, especially our own. We constantly seek ways to stave off aging and mortality. We are marketed endless products to keep us young and vital. We deny our grieving hearts in a rush to move on to something more cheerful. Many of our thoughts are ways to distract us from this reality.

This all comes at great cost to the well-being of our souls. I have sat vigil with the dying, including my mother and my husband's mother, and there is something indescribably holy about those threshold times as someone makes the transition from this life into the Great Mystery.

The desert monks had a keen practice of keeping an awareness of death. Amma Sarah said, "I put my foot out to ascend the ladder, and I place death before my eyes before going up it."[4] Being mindful of our eventual death need not be morbid, but it calls us to always return to that which is essential. In the desert tradition, death is a friend and companion along the journey, assisting us in releasing everything that is not God. St. Benedict writes in his Rule: "Keep death daily before your eyes." This was never meant to be a morbid preoccupation but a profound honoring of the way our mortality can bring us so close to the essential things of life.

St. Francis of Assisi referred to death as "sister" in his famous poem "The Canticle of Creation." Rather than the presence at the end of our lives, death can become a companion along each step, heightening our awareness of life's beauty and calling us toward living more fully. Living with Sister Death calls us to greater freedom and responsibility.

How are we to approach this invitation? What if each morning you awoke with a sense of life's incredible gift, to be alive for another day, and to have another opportunity to love again? What if every time your thoughts turned to tearing yourself down, you remembered just how precious these moments are? Might you start to shift toward cherishing yourself and your life a bit more?

Responses to Death as Gift

Maybe it's time to let go
of thunder, not grasp for edges,
then have to bandage cuts
and bruises, the legacy of glass.

Maybe it's time to break the mold,
toss it into the air, and have the wind
pick up the pieces.

Wear the hats of leading ladies
read the great works of children
whose truth is clear in misspelled words.

Maybe it's time to say "no" instead
of "yes"; "yes" instead of silence.
Take a hand that didn't know it was open,
catching rain in its palm, watering the
grass with its touch.

It's time—time before the ball ends at
    midnight.

—Barbara Flaherty

"What the Body Knows"

I ask my mind, What about death?
Fearfully she peers into the Void.
She sees nothing.
She screams.

I ask my soul, What about death?

She looks at me uncomprehending.
She only yearns for her Beloved.
Her seeking is forever.

I ask my body, What about death?
She gazes at me with tears in her eyes,
Then mutely raises her arms and spirals
Into her dance of dissolution,
Into the curled and coiled embrace
Of the secret Mother Womb.
There she rests, silent.
There she rests, waiting.

—Deborah Delano

able to care
a little
for the
fury
and rage
inside

phew

a
melting

—Linda Pearson

Creative Exploration:
Photography Wisdom Cards

To begin I invite you to let three questions arise for you. Phil Cousineau, author of *The Art of Pilgrimage*, says, "The purpose behind questions is to initiate the quest,"[5] and the poet Rainer Maria Rilke invites us to "live the questions"[6] as a way of dwelling in mystery. Questions point us to thresholds of unknowing and help to move our minds away from the answers they so desperately seek. These questions might be sparked by awareness of your own mortality and preciousness of days or the grace of thresholds all around you. Write your three questions down on separate slips of paper and fold them up so you can't see them.

Release the questions entirely. Go on a contemplative walk, which is a time to walk slowly out in the world and receive images that come to you. Allow twenty to thirty minutes to walk and notice what shimmers for you, what calls you to pay attention. Use a camera to receive a gift of that image.

When you return, choose three photos with which to work. Allow time for free writing in response to the process and what you discovered. Let each element of the image have a voice, speaking from the "I am . . ." After this, spend some time again with each one, this time asking the question, "What wisdom do you have to offer to me?" Allow enough time to fully explore the responses that arise.

Once you have completed this process, number the three photos one, two, and three. Then unfold each of the questions. Match the first one you unfolded to the first photo and so forth with the second and third so that each question accompanies a photo. Do this without planning or looking at the questions. Let this just be an intuitive process.

Then spend some time with each question again, this time listening to the wisdom the corresponding photo offers. See if there is resonance or dissonance. Be curious about any connections. Hold the process lightly. Notice if there is new insight that your mind could not have thought its way through to.

Movement Exploration

Yin Yoga: Dragonfly

For dragonfly pose you begin sitting on the floor with your legs extended out in front of you. Then spread them outward into a V-shape so your legs are still straight and flat on the floor. Very gently roll your spine forward so your upper body hangs over the space between your legs. Most of us will not reach the floor, nor is this our goal. You can use a bolster angled up to support your head if this would feel good. Let your knees bend gently if needed. You can also place folded blankets or blocks under them for more support.

Once you have found a position that you can maintain for a while, bring your attention to your breath. As time passes, notice your thoughts as they arise. Notice if judgments come up, such as voices that feel impatient or doubtful about the value of what you are doing. Maybe the voices remind you that you have too much to do today, so it would be better to skip your practice today.

See if you can allow your time in this pose to be a period of gentle mindfulness, bringing attention to the thoughts that enter your consciousness. See if you might let those thoughts simply drift by rather than grasping onto them. When you notice that you have gone down a rabbit trail of thoughts, gently bring your attention back.

When you have completed the pose, take a few deep breaths to transition out of it. Some gentle backbends and arches to the spine to counterbalance the dragonfly pose can feel good.

Dancing a New Story

If we have particularly painful memories we carry as wounds—such as a family dysfunction, loss or regret, or even a recent frustration—sometimes we can have a sense of being stuck in our own life story. A very powerful transformative tool can be a story of redemption that is based on an InterPlay form.

The idea is that we can change the endings of stories we have experienced to find a more redemptive ending. Essentially, we tell a story that has been cemented into our narrative understanding of ourselves and carries shame or regret, but we add an ending that moves us closer to wholeness. My friend and colleague Kayce Stevens Hughlett had a powerful experience with this:

> My father died in a tragic trucking accident the day after my nineteenth birthday. For years I have carried heavy guilt knowing he tried to call me on my birthday and I was not there to pick up the phone. When I was invited to imaginatively shift a memory, this day rose to the forefront. I resisted for a moment and then allowed myself to imagine answering the phone. I could hear his voice clearly and distinctly. "Happy Birthday, Baby. I love you. How's your day?" Short. Sweet. Simple. I remembered he was a man of few words. With a healing salve, the guilt began to soften and peel away. Through the re-telling, I knew there was no guilt to be had for celebrating my birthday. It was exactly how he would have wanted it.[7]

We can take the experience even deeper by dancing the story, bringing the unfolding of it into our bodies and then letting our bodies direct the way the new ending comes about.

The story of redemption can be especially powerful around body shame we might carry. If we had an experience as a young child, for example, of being told not to dance so wildly, to keep ourselves contained and not so out there, we might imagine how the story would unfold if we hadn't been taught that. We could dance *as if* our childhood were filled with wild and expressive movement and let ourselves have that embodied experience connected with our imagining.

Begin by finding some music that draws you in, perhaps something slow paced and instrumental so you can really access your inner material and listen to how the dance wants to unfold without being carried away by external words and rhythms. You could also explore this in silence. Or perhaps there are some songs from your childhood that you would love to dance freely to now. Tune into what would feel most supportive.

Imagine the story, and at the point where it takes a destructive turn, ask your body to show you a new ending and allow the dance to unfold from this awareness. Let yourself have this experience without trying to figure out its meaning.

A few words of caution here: Remember to stay connected to your breath as an anchor and safe resource. When you feel yourself coming up against your limits, step away and come back at another time or seek support for this exploration, perhaps in the company of a dear friend or wise counselor.

Reflection Questions

- What are the stories and patterns of thought you are discovering?
- When you begin to pay attention, are you able to notice when those thoughts arise and consciously create a new story or thought pattern?
- What happens when you listen to your intuition? Are there are images, colors, or symbols that arise?

Closing Blessing

Body Psalm for Intuitives

there are worlds beyond the one
you live in
beneath you in the magma
beside you in the wind
inside you in dreams

layers exist within the archaeology
of your heart's knowing
sometimes it only takes a drop
of truth which resonates
to remember there is another way

where the answer to issues
is not another meeting
or change of direction, drive or data
but a turning to the inward pool of
I N T U I T I V I A
an intuitive's call

the researcher may look for data
but there is a data of the body
spiritsongs of the cells
beckoning the child in you
to come alive

there is a physical core one needs to stand
but an internal core
will light you through the shadows
break you into humility
and glow beyond
what is known

—Celeste Snowber

Chapter 6

Exile and Lament:
The Vulnerability of the Body

That I may be filled with them.
That I may be emptied by them.

That they may challenge
my silence.
That they may lead me
to speech.

That I may name each one.
That I may be named by each one.

That they may teach me
of my sorrow.
That they may lead me
to my strength.

—Jan Richardson, "Blessing of the Tears"

As I mentioned in the first chapter, when I was twenty-one years old I was diagnosed with rheumatoid arthritis, an autoimmune disease that had caused severe degeneration for my mother for many years. By the time she was in her fifties, she had multiple joint replacements, including both hips and knees, and had her ankles and wrists fused. In the last few years of her life she got around in an electric wheelchair, which actually gave her so much of her independence back after years of struggling to walk.

It was a devastating diagnosis for me because I had seen through my mother the daily effects and profound struggles caused by rheumatoid arthritis, and my mother didn't develop the disease until her midthirties. Once my pain and inflammation was somewhat controlled with disease-modifying drugs, I didn't think to slow myself down at all. I was young and at the beginning of my adulthood, full of promise and possibility. In my midtwenties I worked at a Catholic high school teaching and working in campus ministry, offering retreats to students and faculty. I thoroughly enjoyed my work, but it was a demanding job that took its toll on my vulnerable body. Three years later my fatigue and pain had worsened to the point where I needed to take a year off from work and go on disability.

I was in pain much of the time, but adding to the pain was my grief and anger at why this was happening as well as the burden I felt every time someone new asked me what I did for a living. It was a common question, and as I did not look sick, each time I struggled to name what was happening to me, often to the great discomfort of the other person. People don't want to be reminded of the body's vulnerability, and in an effort to control this situation, they suggested all kinds of remedies I should try, often with the underlying implication that I simply wasn't trying hard enough. Church people especially desired to be helpful by reminding me that God must have a plan (please don't ever say this to someone suffering). It was quite exhausting dealing with other people's expectations, and I was too young at the time to be able to set proper boundaries.

One day, however, at church, I received the same dreaded question, but this time, when I shared with the woman that I was on disability for a medical condition, taking some time off to rest, she exclaimed, "Oh, you are on a *sabbatical!*" And with that simple word, I felt my entire body soften and move into a place of greater relief. Suddenly I had a word that could honor this place I found myself in by rooting me in an ancient practice and tradition of rest.

Her statement to me was the turning point in many ways for how I came to be in relationship with my illness. I struggled much of the time, wanting to feel better, wanting my energy restored. But when I could embrace that my body needed sabbath time, when I stopped resisting the truth of my experience, so much ease returned to my heart.

When I went on disability, my husband and I moved to a small town near Sacramento, California, called Woodland where he got a job as a youth minister. It was at the little health club there that I began my practice of yoga. This was a few years before yoga became available everywhere. I still remember my teacher with fondness; Tracie Sage was trained in the Kripalu tradition, which is a gentle form of yoga with emphasis on breath and listening to your body. I feel fortunate that she was my first formal experience as she offered me a doorway into my body through breath and gentle poses. She helped me to find a place of ease in my body even if everything else I tried to do caused me pain. Three mornings each week I would arrive for her class and then go for a swim and sit in the sauna: all things that felt good physically. It was a small respite and place of deep healing in that time of pain and grief.

I also tried, as much as I could, to make room for the grief. With the reframing of my experience as sabbath, I lessened some of my resistance to the situation I found myself in. I let myself feel terrible and weep and mourn, and I also discovered that even in the midst of so much pain, there were still many moments of joy and laughter as well.

I later returned to graduate school to work on my PhD at my own pace, something I had always wanted to pursue, but the fear and uncertainty of whether I would be able to work, whether I would be well enough to show up for a job consistently, had always prevented me before. Would I be able to fulfill my deep desires for meaningful work?

I was very fortunate that in my early thirties a new medication was developed that offered me so much relief from pain. I continue to take it now, sixteen years later, and am grateful every day for the quality of life it helps to provide. I still have residual pain in my hands and feet from joint deterioration that happened twenty years ago. I still have to monitor my energy and be mindful, but overall, the difference between how I feel now and then is remarkable.

Even after starting the new medication and finding relief, for many years I still lived with the story that I couldn't work full time because of my disease. I had come to accept this as truth, making it hard to begin to shift the narrative and see that my capacities were increasing, that I was able to work longer and longer hours.

Woven through this whole experience over many years has been a long journey of coming home to my body. To say I felt in exile when first diagnosed would be a vast understatement. I felt betrayed and full of grief, resisting how things were at every turn. Coming home—which is always a process—has not been so much about finding the right medications, although that certainly has helped. Coming home has happened by honoring what is most nourishing to my body through cooking, herbalism, and movement; by learning to listen to my body's wisdom; by not making apologies for taking extravagant care of this physical vessel that allows me to be present in the world; and by allowing the range of feeling and emotion to flow through me and have their full expression. While I've found much healing, I continue to weep and mourn my losses, as much as I can, without apology.

Embracing Grief and Lament

I invited you in chapter 3 to consider savoring all of your experience. Does this mean the grief and sorrow as well? Can I practice radical hospitality to the whole of myself, even the parts that bring pain? Can I pause right now and notice how I feel without trying to change it, without rushing to judge or analyze why I am feeling this way?

And what about the deep desires you were encouraged to get in touch with in chapter 4? What if they are thwarted because of great loss or illness? What if there is a real physical reason you can't move forward into your great dream?

Each one of us carries grief, a sorrow that has perhaps gone unexpressed or been stifled or numbed. Each of us has been touched by pain and suffering at some time. Yet we live in a culture that tells us to move on, to get over it, to shop or drink our way through sorrow, or to fill our moments with the chatter of television and Internet so that we never have to face the silent desert of our hearts. It is the same kind of attitude that forces us to answer, "Fine," when others ask how we are, though we really aren't.

Why do we work so hard to resist our tears? Jesus wept. We see him in John's gospel shedding tears over the death of his friend Lazarus. In Luke's gospel we see him weeping over the city of Jerusalem because of their indifference. He cries out from the Cross in lament, "My God, my God, why have you forsaken me?" (Mt 27:46).

This is where the profound wisdom in our tradition of lament enters. The Hebrew Scriptures are filled with this prayer of crying out to God. Lament gives form and voice to our grief, a space to wail and name what is not right in the world in the context of prayer.

The Protestant theologian Walter Brueggemann writes about the need for lament in his book *The Prophetic Imagination*. He says that people can only dare to envision a new reality when they've been able to grieve, to scream out, and to let loose the cry that has been stuck in their throats for so long. That cry, that expression of that grief, says Brueggemann, "is the most visceral announcement that things are not right."[1] Only then can we begin to "to nurture, nourish, and evoke a consciousness and perception alternative to the consciousness and perception of the dominant culture around us."[2] John Philip Newell writes in *A New Harmony: The Spirit, the Earth, and the Human Soul* that one of the rules St. Columba of Iona wrote was "to pray 'until thy tears come.'"[3] When tears flow, something very deep within us stirs. Prayer is about getting in touch with the deepest dimension of our being.

The prayer of lament is first and foremost truth telling; it begins by challenging the way things are. Lament declares that something is not right in the world. This pain, this suffering, should not be. It helps us to name the lies we have been living and participating in.

Lament opens us up to a new vision of how God is present to our suffering. We call on the God who weeps with us, whose groans are our own, and we express our hope in God's tender care.

Lament is a form of resistance: We allow ourselves to be present to God in our brokenness and resist the cultural imperative to be strong and hold it all together. We resist cultural practices of denying death through our worship of eternal youth. We stop pretending everything is okay and put an end to worshiping the status quo.

Lament puts us in solidarity with those who are suffering and schools us in compassion. Only when we have become familiar with the landscape of our own pain can we then enter into the suffering of another. Lament moves us beyond our own narrow perspectives.

In the prayer of lament we help give voice to the oppressed, to hidden suffering, and to the suffering in silence that happens because pain takes our language away. Gathered together we say that the pain is heard, that it is valid. Our community votes with its tears that there is suffering worth weeping over.

Our focus has been on lament over the exile we have experienced from our bodies. We can cry out that we must be exiled no longer. Lament speaks the truth that our bodies are sources of immense wisdom and we will not be separated from them any longer. We will no longer live under the illusion that we can control our bodies through busyness and denial.

Embracing Paradox and Mystery

> To explore a body symptom is to enter it, as it has entered us, and to partake in a sacred mystery. It is with the greatest respect and humility that we undertake this task.
>
> —Rose-Emily Rothenberg, *The Jewel in the Wound*

I don't mean to leave you with the impression that opening to grief and allowing rest has relieved me of all physical pain. I still struggle with chronic pain that flares for various reasons and sometimes none at all. I still feel fatigue if I work too hard. Sometimes we fall into the trap of believing that if we just do everything right, we will be cured. We can become fixated on magical thinking. We can do everything we can to support ourselves in healing, which is an invitation to embrace wholeness even when we don't feel fully well, and still not always feel as comfortable in our bodies as we would hope.

This continues to be a journey. Instead of seeking to be fixed in some way, I seek what is most nourishing. Instead of resisting the pain and pushing forward, I try to yield to it, to breathe in love to the part of me hurting. This isn't always possible—sometimes I am teaching and have to teach through the pain—but the more I can offer this when I am unwell, the more nurtured I feel and the more my body responds. Instead of buying into the cultural models of body acceptance, I practice bringing my body love each day through attention, care, and listening.

Being with the body and listening to her wisdom can offer so much grace. We are seeking not a cure but healing. Healing happens on a soul level as an integration and a welcoming in of all that has been rejected in us.

There are many reasons for illness. Sometimes it arises because we are running ourselves ragged and we need to stop; the symptom is an invitation to listen deeply and confront our own patterns of violence to ourselves. However, sometimes illness is caused by the wounds of our ancestors that we carry forward. Rheumatoid arthritis definitely has a strong genetic predisposition, as do many other illnesses. Sometimes we carry the unresolved conflicts and traumas of generations in our bodies. In those cases, we can only learn to be exquisitely gentle with ourselves and give voice to their silenced stories.

Sometimes illness is caused by the terrible poisoning of the earth: our drinking water carries traces of prescription drugs, our food is often sprayed with chemicals, and we are exposed to toxins from car emissions and other industrial waste. These are all reasons for lament. I believe that some of us were born in more vulnerable bodies than others and have become the "canaries in the coal mine," which was the practice of sending canaries down into mines to test whether toxic gases had been released. Some of us show signs sooner than others of our environmental recklessness.

Ultimately, I think illness demands that we embrace the great mystery at the heart of life: Why is there suffering at all? As organic beings, why is decay and death woven into our very fabric? There are no simple answers to these questions; they are a mystery to be lived.

No matter the cause, listening to the symptoms can offer us wisdom. We can hear the call to slow down and nourish our bodies well. We might hear the invitation to bring compassion to the great struggles of our ancestors. We might hear the earth crying through our bodies and the summons to be more mindful of living lightly.

Illness can be a soulful journey that brings great wisdom to our lives as it offers an intimate connection to our vulnerability and mortality and a reminder that one day we will breathe our last breath and return to the earth. Illness invites us into a deeper presence with the gifts we have and into simplicity, calling us to what is most essential. Pain and disease strip away all that is not important in our lives. In many indigenous cultures, the shaman is one who experiences a great descent into the underworld through serious illness. The shaman was often the "wounded healer" of a tribe, the one who had faced great suffering, endured, and emerged able to offer wisdom to the community about living with challenges.

This is not to say that these things happen to teach us lessons. I think that is too simplistic an equation and often a damaging one for those struggling with pain. God does not give us these illnesses to teach us something, but God is already present with us in the sweet landscape of our bodies, inviting us to listen for the wisdom being revealed.

The central question we are invited to ask is this: Can my body be ill or in pain and beautiful and whole at the same time? Our bodies invite us to hold this paradox.

Ally on the Journey: Rachel

> Thus says the LORD,
> A voice is heard in Ramah,
> lamentation and bitter weeping.
> Rachel is weeping for her children;
> she refuses to be comforted for her children,
> because they are no more.
>
> —Jeremiah 31:15

After my mother died suddenly in 2003, I was overcome with terrible grief, and this scripture passage became my anchor and sustenance. I was so moved that Rachel did not allow herself to be comforted in the midst of a loss so inconsolable. Often when we are in the midst of grief, others want to move us to a place of hope or comfort. It takes strength and wisdom to resist and allow ourselves the fierceness of our loss. Rachel's story gave me permission to not suppress the grief. Sometimes there are losses for which there is no consolation.

You might consider welcoming Rachel in to stand in the growing community of women we have standing with us in this journey of embodiment. Imagine her taking her place alongside Hildegard of Bingen, Sophia, the Desert Mothers, the woman from the Song of Songs, and Eve.

There is something deeply physical about a grief that is allowed its freedom and expression. Wailing comes from our limbs.

Practice: Keening and the Gift of Tears

There is a tradition in Ireland, sadly now almost gone, of keening at funerals. Keening is a vocal lament, usually practiced by women, through a series of improvisational songs. Keening also involved the whole body in kneeling, rocking, and clapping. It was a powerful and embodied rite of passage, offering a physical release for those in grief. We have references to the practice as early as the seventh century, but keening was sadly later banned by the Catholic Church around the seventeenth century. Some women became professional keeners, and clergy banned it as a result. I find keening to be a powerful embodied expression of grief. When we experience profound loss, it is a loss that comes through us both body and soul. Keening honors this expression that arises through our limbs and voice.

Irish scholars have written that keening happened not only at funerals but also at other occasions, such as when children left home to emigrate away or during the potato famine. It is a ritual way of making space for the ancient embodied cry that rises up when we are plunged into loss. My invitation to you is to welcome in the grief your body holds. As always, return to your breathing when needed, know your own limits, and come back to this exercise at a later time if now feels like too much. Seek support and someone in whom you can confide to process any feelings that arise.

Begin by telling yourself you are in a safe space and you have the strength and resources to be present. If you feel safe enough and have enough privacy, consider adding your voice into your prayer. Continue to work with the breath, savoring with your senses, welcoming in your feelings as they arise, and quieting your judgments.

Play music if it is a helpful container and allows safe space for expression of grief. See if you can be aware when old stories about stuckness arise, and let them go in favor of listening for the body's actual experience beneath. Notice what grief your body wants to express.

Perhaps the grief you carry is over illness and disease in your body right now; perhaps it is the loss of someone you loved or their struggles with illness. Maybe the grief that arises comes from recognizing how far into exile you have gone with your body and how far away the journey home feels.

Go tenderly and gently. Remember, this is just the beginning of a journey.

Meditation: Body Examen

> Our mourning compels us to name our sorrows, to name our losses, to name our wounds inflicted and received. Our grieving beckons us, too, to name our causes for joy, to name our dreams and longings. Our mourning invites us beyond our own heart's desires into the heart of a world as fragile as glass, as easily broken, and brimming with the promise of healing.
>
> —Jan Richardson, *In Wisdom's Path*

Move into a quiet and meditative space. Find a comfortable seated position, and let your breath deepen for a few cycles. Move into a place of rest and release, where you do not need to make any effort. Simply allow whatever images want to rise to come.

Reflect back on your life and remember a time when you felt good in your body, when you felt a sense of aliveness and joy or pleasure without shame. Notice what memory arises in response to this invitation. Savor the experience. Let yourself enter into it again with all of your senses. Be present to all the facets of this moment, and feel it in your body again as much as possible.

Offer gratitude for this gift of aliveness and body delight. Take three full and slow deep breaths.

Reflect back again on your life, and this time remember an experience when it felt very difficult to be in your body, whether because of pain, overwhelming grief, or another emotion. Continuing to stay connected to your breath, welcome in that experience again so that you can imagine it for a moment. Let yourself enter into it and feel whatever comes, knowing that you can step out of the memory at any time and return to the present moment.

Soften your heart and see if you might be able to offer forgiveness for any way that your body felt as if it betrayed you or to yourself for any self-judgment of lack of compassion at the time. Know that you can bring this gift to yourself now.

Release this experience and then allow a few full breaths to return to this moment now. Be very tender and gentle with yourself. Write down any reflections or things you noticed during that experience.

Creative Exploration: Writing a Prayer of Lament

The psalms are filled with prayers of lament, the cry that something is not right, the anguished voices before God. Allow yourself space to write your own prayer of naming and truth telling. Let this be a prayer that refuses to be silenced, refuses to say that everything is okay. Cry out against the voices that tell you your body is anything but beautiful.

Let this be a poem expressing something that brings the gift of tears for you. It can be filled with anger or grief. If there is fear over this writing being found and that creates a barrier to entering into the exercise, know that you do not have to keep the writing. You can release it through burning it, burying it in the earth, or running it through the shredder. If writing feels like a barrier to expressing this prayer, consider creating a piece of art that becomes your prayer or a dancing a lament.

If you choose to write, this structure of a psalm of lament can be a loose guide:

- *Address to God*: How do you call upon the divine presence of God?
- *Complaint*: What is your lament and cry of pain?
- *Affirmation of trust*: Have you had an experience of God meeting you in your pain before? Draw on this memory to experience a sense of companionship in your grief.
- *Petition*: What is your deepest desire from God? What do you want for the earth?
- *Assurance of being heard*: What do you need from God to feel witnessed?
- *Vow of praise*: What can you promise or offer to God on behalf of your longing?
- *Hymn or blessing*: Is there something for which you can express gratitude, wonder, or delight?

Responses to Writing a Lament

> "Cry aloud to the Lord!
> O wall of daughter Zion!
> Let tears stream down like a torrent
> day and night!
> Give yourself no rest,
> your eyes no respite!"
> (Lam 2:18)

For you have scorned your beauteous
    temple,
Your shrine of flesh and form
You have pushed, cajoled her to her limit
Until she lies spent and weary and
    forlorn

You have discarded the rising and falling
The sacred pauses of fullness and rest

You have lit your streets with all-night
    neon
Where neither person nor creature may
    rest

You have plundered the earth of its riches
Believed that only this generation may
    be fed
You have dismissed the cries of the seas
Have tried Gaia's patience and tested her
    wrath

You have eaten and witnessed your full
You have tasted and touched too much
You have lost your sense of "enough"
Now all your senses betray you

You have lingered too long with old loves
And have missed the big heart before
    you
You have believed the lies of false
    prophets
And worshiped the easy, the instant, the
    young.

You store your grief in your bones
Choke your lungs with unshed tears
You deceive your eyes with the ad breaks
You chase the coffee, the grind

Your children pluck buds before blossom
Pour scorn on your traditions and
    prayers
You stammer defenses of the old ways
And hear the echoes of disbelief from
    within

You are pierced by the cries of the
    children
Syrian, Malian, Sudanese,
Eyes of despair and of longing haunt
    your sleep
Interrupting your grace before meals

You know not the way forward through
    this wasteland
Fear your resources no match for the task
You call upon the Lord of your making
Sit Shiva in surrender and collapse

"I called upon your name, O LORD,
from the depths of the pit;
You heard my plea, 'Do not close your
    ear
to my cry for help, but give me relief!'
You came near when I called on you;
you said, 'Do not fear!'"
(Lam 3:55–57)

—Judith King

Holy One, Mysterious Beauty,
I cry now, tears rolling down my face,
lump in the throat, holding my breath
    unconsciously.
These signs of sadness and grief are all
    too familiar, but right now there are
    no words.
This happens too, this I also know.
Hidden suffering. Silent suffering. Pain
    for which I have no words.

Something hurts deep inside, way down
    in a dark abyss,
a never-ending well into darkness, the
    night.
I whimper and cry without knowing
    why, a pain so great I am numb.
My stomach clenches.
Breathe, sweet one, breathe.
The tears turn to sobbing.
Why am I crying?
What pain, what injustice, does my body
    hold so deep below the surface of my
    consciousness?? What pain is buried
    so as to never be found?!
I cry out to you, dear Lord, for help! For
    understanding
For some sort of healing balm that can
    reach down and soothe me, give me
    words!!
For now, there are none.
Although I sense this is the foundational
    wound,
the wound that began in the womb,
the wound of absence,
the wound of indifference,
the wound of no love.
Leaving me with a felt-sense that I wasn't
    supposed to be here,
I didn't have a right to live.
Making me so small inside, I barely
    breathed, I barely moved.
Hidden behind my vibrant, loud
    personality was a tiny, tiny soul,
waiting to be loved into being.

A sweet, generous soul, buried in order
    to survive.
A fracture, a fissure, right through my
    heart.
I grieve for that baby. I scream for that
    baby!
My God, my God, why did you forsake
    me?!
Why did I get left out of Eden?

—Liz Morris

Sadness comes to visit
often lately wearing
a large Victorian hat,
its brim tilted down shading
the stories in her eyes, a reminder
of other days whose time
is not yet finished.

Sadness, thy garb is pale,
demur, yet cool
with loneliness.

You sit in the wide
wicker chair, poise
for tea, waiting
for conversation to continue
from the past.

Then, talk about the weather.

How long will you linger this time,
gauging how to be polite, listening
to the counting of the mantle clock?

A muffled pass of whispers
and the tea cup shatters
on the empty shadow.

—Barbara Flaherty

I know grief.
I have wept with it.
It has made me numb.
I have lived in a glass cube
begging to be free
with shards of glass piercing me
i have breathed
i have grieved
i have lost
friends
home
an active life I loved
in the Florida sunshine
i am alone
making a new life
in a place full of creativity
making new friends
slowly, ever so slowly.
My body withers with the winter winds
and pain becomes me
and I breathe
and I breathe
and I breathe
and I grieve
for the energy consumed
in just breathing.

—Wendy Jo Wisniewski

Movement Exploration

Yin Yoga: Child's Pose

Child's pose is meant to be a very restful pose. Often in a yoga class it is offered as an option, in addition to corpse pose, to come into if you need a pause. As we work through this tender material on grief, let this pose be a gentle holding of your child self. Come to your knees and then drape the front of your body forward toward the floor. If your belly makes this pose uncomfortable, widen your knees. I personally find this version easier and more relaxing.

As you sink into the pose, allow some slow breaths to steady and center you. Become aware of places of holding or tension, and bring your breath to those spots to ease the tightness. Scan your body to see if there are any sensations that need tending. Let this be an extraordinarily gentle time. Tears may rise up; if so, allow them to flow with no holding back.

After child's pose you may want to come forward to lie on your belly, with one cheek on the mat, closing your eyes and resting for a few moments.

Dance on Behalf Of

I invite you into another InterPlay movement practice, this time the Dance on Behalf Of. This is one of my favorite forms as it can help me move beyond my own concerns and connect to the struggles of others in solidarity through dance. This can be a beautiful experience of offering your dance as a prayer for another and discovering dance as a vessel for a wide range of prayers.

To begin, decide on someone or something you want to offer a dance on behalf of. This could be for another person who is suffering right now, for yourself in a time when you were younger and really struggling, or even on behalf of a current experience of physical struggle. You are not being asked to somatize the suffering of others. You may choose to lift it up to the Divine and dance as if the prayer were being answered.

Take exquisite care of yourself in this process. Keep connected to your breath. You can always move back to stillness at any time or step out of the dance entirely if you feel overwhelmed with emotion. Offer the prayer back to the Divine.

Find a meditative piece of music to hold the dance, and as the music begins, let go of any thoughts you might have about directing the dance, and enter into how your body longs to move. Just hold the person or situation you are dancing for gently in your thoughts and follow your body's impulse.

When the song is done, allow some time to rest into stillness and feel whatever is flowing through you. Then write down anything you noticed in a journal. Consider seeking the support of a trusted soul friend with whom to share the fruits of this practice.

Reflection Questions

- What are the great losses of your life that live in your body's memory?
- What happens when you view tears as a gift and a threshold to new intimacy with the Divine?
- What are the laments you still want to explore and enter into?

Closing Blessing

BodyPsalm for Body Rest

You have gone through
a massive shift, your body is calling
you to bodyrest
it is a time to take in the support
beneath your feet
encompassing your world
from every small and large place—
friends, family, beloveds,
practitioners: medical and alternative
and the wider embrace
of the divine—the great Love.
We are each called to surrender
to the change that continues
to inhabit our bodyspirits
as uncomfortable as they are
strength runs through you
and has been building
from each bending towards
the demands of life transitions
you have already
leaned into these ruptures.
Now is the time to lean
into the love that is with you
and let your body receive
a transfusion of beginnings
here in this change to your cells
is the invitation
to a new chapter of health
altered from before
yet an honored passage

to a season of clarity
where you will be free
to archive the beauty of your life
and venture into the
dawn of desire within
your loss will be your entrance
to a new way of being.
Drink in the support of care
and t r u s t in
the landscape of your own heart
beckoning you
to the shore of wellness
breathing you from the inside out
and most of all—be patient towards all
that is not known
and rest your head in
the pillow of comfort
where you are held
from a much deeper place
and know your pain
is stitching you to healing
where you are being
re-created to enter
the magnificence of your own life.

—Celeste Snowber

Chapter 7

Holiness Made Flesh: The Incarnation and Embodied Life

We awaken in Christ's body
as Christ awakens our bodies,
and my poor hand is Christ, He enters
my foot, and is infinitely me.

I move my hand, and wonderfully
my hand becomes Christ, becomes all of Him
(for God is indivisibly
whole, seamless in His Godhood).

I move my foot, and at once
He appears like a flash of lightning.
Do my words seem blasphemous?—Then
open your heart to Him

and let yourself receive the one
who is opening to you so deeply.
For if we genuinely love Him,
we wake up inside Christ's body

where all our body, all over,
every most hidden part of it,
is realized in joy as Him,
and He makes us, utterly, real,

and everything that is hurt, everything
that seemed to us dark, harsh, shameful,
maimed, ugly, irreparably
damaged, is in Him transformed

and recognized as whole, as lovely,
and radiant in His light
he awakens as the Beloved
in every last part of our body.

—Symeon the New Theologian

In my flesh I shall see God.

—Job 19:26

Embodiment can be terribly inconvenient: flesh, blood, sweat, mucus, saliva, muscles, ligaments, bones, organs, and hair can all feel like a burden at times or something you want to control. Sadly, the Christian tradition has sometimes depicted the body as a prison from which to escape rather than a sanctuary in which to dwell and flourish. And yet the heart of this path is the belief that God became flesh—that holiness infused flesh and blood and experienced both the pain and delight of embodied life, joining us in the vulnerability and mortality with which we must all wrestle.

As we are discovering, the intentional journey into the body is full of fear and trembling as well as delight and pleasure. Incarnation is more than just being in the body; it is also allowing the body to be the very vessel of connection, service, and sacred encounter. Without our bodies we would have no way of interacting with others in the world.

We were created as body and soul, and this embodied existence is declared very good right in the story of the creation. The story of exile from the garden of Eden has been interpreted on one level as being about our woundedness in body as Eve would now have pain in childbirth as a consequence of sin. But perhaps we might shift our perspective and see this as a wisdom tale about our alienation from the fullness of ourselves. Perhaps the pain arises as a consequence of our self-imposed exile rather than as a punishment. Maybe it is illuminating how far away from home we have traveled.

"Self-objectification" is a term to describe when we no longer regard our bodies as an integral part of our selves. Instead, we view them as a marketable collection of parts that need to be modified to increase sexual desirability or, at the very least, for acceptance by the larger culture.

The more we strive to achieve external standards of beauty and acceptability by manipulating our image, the more distant we feel from who we really are. It is our bodies as they are right now, not in some imagined fantasy of how they could or should be, that offer us the path to grace, wisdom, and the divine unfolding of our own unique gifts.

Jesus' humanity is described again and again in the gospels. One of the last things he says in his life is that he is thirsty. In the story of the Samaritan woman by the well, he sits down because he is tired. He weeps over Jerusalem, and he overturns the tables of the money changers in the Temple in anger. He is unable to carry his cross by himself because of sheer exhaustion. When stabbed in the side, he bleeds. And his last act of sharing with his disciples is the breaking of bread and drinking of wine. Even the resurrection narratives read during the season of Easter point to an embodied Christ who still bears his wounds, who is revealed in the breaking of the bread once again, and who gathers an abundance of fish from the sea so that all may be nourished.

Richard Rohr describes the incarnation not as something that happened "in Bethlehem two thousand years ago." He writes,

> That is just when some of us started taking it seriously. The incarnation actually happened approximately 14.5 billion years ago with a moment that we now call "The Big Bang." That is when God actually decided to materialize and to expose who God is. This alone provides any solid basis for reverence, universal sacrality, and our attempts to form a spiritual ecology that transcends groups and religions. Two thousand years ago marked the human

incarnation of God in Jesus, we Christians believe, but before that there was the first and original incarnation through light, water, land, sun, moon, stars, plants, trees, fruit, birds, serpents, cattle, fish, and "every kind of wild beast," according to our Judeo-Christian creation story (Genesis 1:3–25). This was the "Cosmic Christ" through which God has "let us know the mystery of his purpose, the hidden plan he so kindly made from the beginning in Christ" (Ephesians 1:9).[1]

Then we have the words above of Symeon the New Theologian, an Eastern Orthodox monk from the ninth and tenth centuries, with the invitation to see that every part of ourselves that feels "dark, harsh, shameful, maimed, ugly, irreparably damaged" is transformed, is seen as whole. Christ dwells within us, which is to say that the one who brings the Divine and human together is present within us both body and soul.

Trusting the Body

Rabbi Shalom Noah Barzovsky, the previous Slonimer Rebbe, teaches that there are three kinds of *emunah* (elemental trust): trusting mind, trusting heart, and trusting body. And the highest of these is *emunat ha-evarim*, trusting with one's limbs, where deep trust penetrates every fibre of one's being. The classic example he offers is the crossing of the Sea of Reeds. In that moment of leaping, he writes (in his commentary on parashat Beshalach), the children of Israel trusted fully in the One, and therefore the holy spirit rested upon them and sang in them (this is a Hebrew pun—התרש / *shartah*, rested, relates aurally to הריש / *shirah*, song) and song burst forth not only from their lips but in their very limbs.

—Rachel Barenblat,
"Embodied Trust," at velveteenrabbi.blogs.com

Emunat ha-evarim—trusting with one's limbs—is an amazing image. As we move through this world, what are the practices that help us to cultivate this profound sense of knowing, trusting, and being that our bodies offer? We are not encouraged to trust our bodies in this culture, for they forever need improving. We can buy an endless variety of products and programs geared solely at responding to the message that our bodies are somehow not good enough, not beautiful enough, and not wise enough on their own. This undermining of the body works in so many subtle ways.

Several years ago I trained to teach yoga. I began the program because I have practiced yoga for many years and longed to dive more deeply into it. I expected to fall in love with my own body even more in the process; what I didn't expect was how much I would fall in love with other people's bodies as well. As I walked around the studio and students were in their various poses, I saw the incredible variety in body types, shapes, sizes, flexibility, and bone structure. My training involves hands-on adjustments, which are less about fixing a pose and more about either offering a deeper experience of it or providing a sense of loving presence with a student through a shoulder rub or simply laying my hands on their backs, always with permission.

When students are in *savasana*, or corpse pose, which is always the final pose in any physical yoga practice, I go around and place my hands gently on their heads one at a time and offer a silent blessing for them and their bodies. I don't know most of their stories, so I ask for healing in whatever is keeping them from being fully alive and fully present to their beautiful physical selves.

When I lived in Seattle, Washington, one of my favorite places was a Korean women's spa where you paid an entry fee and could then spend hours soaking in various warm pools and lying in infrared sauna rooms and steam rooms. Clothing was not allowed in the spa, and everyone was naked and wearing the same silly shower cap. Soon you would forget your self-consciousness because the variety of bodies there was vast and beautiful. You would see scars and tattoos, thin bodies and curvy bodies. Everyone was there to offer solace and nourishment to their physical being. It was such a rare place of communal slowing down together.

Theologian James Nelson writes, "We do not just use words. We *are* words. . . . In Christ we are redefined as body words of love, and such body life in us is the radical sign of God's love for the world and of the divine immediacy in the World."[2] Body words of love. That phrase takes my breath away. This is the heart of the incarnation. If God becomes flesh, it must be to become a vessel of love in the world. This is where our trust might arise. How do I allow my very body to become the fullest expression of love and tenderness in the world, both toward others and toward myself? This body has its aches and its loveliness. This body has experienced searing pain. And this body will one day become dust but also sprang from my mother in a burst of desire for life.

In all the attention we give to the perfection of the body in our culture, we undermine our capacity to become body words of love, to allow our care for the world to become embodied in the smallest action, in each moment of attention and care. We forget that we are called to both the joy and the sorrow woven together. No surgery can remove our mortality. No procedure can remind us of our sheer giftedness. The effect of our obsessions with our bodies is that we grow in our distrust of our physical selves.

St. Gregory Palamas (1296–1359), an orthodox monk who later became an archbishop, upheld the doctrine that the human body played an important part in prayer rooted in the incarnation; that is, the whole person, united in body and soul, was created in the image of God, and Christ, by taking a human body at the incarnation, has "made the flesh an inexhaustible source of sanctification."[3]

I am in love with this image. What if our bodies truly were an "inexhaustible source of sanctification" and we treated them as such? To sanctify is to bless or make holy, to set apart for sacred use. To consider our bodies a blessing is another way to become "body words of love."

"The Soft Animal of Your Body"

Do you have a body? Don't sit on the porch!
Go out and walk in the rain!

—Kabir

In Mary Oliver's poem "Wild Geese" she has this stunning line: "You only have to let the soft animal of your body love what it loves." What a beautiful reminder that our bodies are animal in nature, with fundamental needs for food, water, movement, rest, and touch that can't be satisfied any other way.

Even more amazing is to consider this in light of the incarnation. Sometimes I wonder if we view the incarnation as the spiritualizing of flesh, when perhaps it might be more helpful to consider it the fleshing of spirit. It is a subtle difference, but rather than trying to elevate our bodies to some "higher" realm, I think the direction of our attention should perhaps be more downward, more into the earthiness of our physical selves. Our spirit becomes rooted and requires the sustenance of earthly life for it to thrive.

The soft animal of your body is vulnerability. Our needs make us dependent and not completely in control. There is such tenderness in this soft place, like the soft belly of a dog turned up to receive love and affection. We are often so critical of our bellies with ubiquitous advertisements for six-pack abs. But what if those rock-hard abdominals were just another form of armoring? What if we could learn to really love and treasure our soft places as a sign of our animal nature? I wonder if God experienced this impulse through the vessel of Jesus' body?

There is a beautiful German film by director Wim Wenders called *Wings of Desire* about two angels who act as witnesses to humanity and long for the experience of being embodied. They talk about how it would be to feed the cat and get newsprint on your fingers, to feel the glorious weight of being in a body. In the same way, Kabir calls us to remember that having a body means walking out in the rain and awakening to the pleasures of embodied life to really feel what it is like to have a body.

Ally on the Journey: The Woman Who Anointed Jesus

A woman in the city, who was a sinner, having learned that he was eating in the Pharisee's house, brought an alabaster jar of ointment. She stood behind him at his feet, weeping, and began to bathe his feet with her tears and to dry them with her hair. Then she continued kissing his feet and anointing them with the ointment.

—Luke 7:37–38

We invite another wise woman guide to be present with us on this journey. She is the woman of whom Jesus spoke these words: "Truly I tell you, wherever this good news is proclaimed in the whole world, what she has done will be told in remembrance of her" (Mt 26:13). Her story appears in all four gospels.

She is introduced in other translations as the "town harlot": the writer already trying to give us a certain impression of her. She is perhaps one who has been shunned by her community, marginalized, ostracized, and rejected. Likely she herself is hurting.

But rather than believe what others think of her or allow that to curtail her, she steps forward in a bold and extravagant act. She listens to her heart and allows the tears to flow. She offers the fullness of herself to Jesus because she knows this act is all that matters in that moment. And she is received with generous grace by him.

Not only does she want to have an encounter with him, but she also desires a moment of physical intimacy and touch. She knows the holiness of the body and acts from this wisdom.

We can call upon her to help us with our own embrace of the incarnation. Perhaps we might anoint ourselves with oil as a way of honoring the sacredness of our flesh. Invite her presence to accompany you and remind you of your own goodness.

Practice: Humility and Remembering Our Earthiness

The word *humility* is derived from *humus*, which means "earth." Humility is at heart about being well grounded and rooted. It is about welcoming in those experiences that create a sense of resistance in us. Humility is also about truth telling and radical self-honesty. It is about celebrating the gifts we have been uniquely given in service of others as well as recognizing our limitations and woundedness.

Humility demands that we also celebrate our blessings as a part of truth telling. It teaches us to recognize that our gifts are not of our own making but are gifts we receive and hold in trust to give to our communities. Our gifts are not for ourselves alone. We are called to create not for our own satisfaction but to participate in the cocreation of a more just and beautiful world.

Humility is about remembering our earthiness and our human limitations. Humility reminds us that we are called not to be all things to all people but to nurture our unique gifts and to recognize that self-care is good stewardship of those gifts. Honoring our limits as creatures can be deeply liberating. Giving up our demanding inner perfectionism can be freeing. How often do I resist beginning a creative project because of my fear that it will not live up to the image in my mind? Humility invites me to release those expectations and enter into the call of my gift, knowing that my call may look very different from my imagining. Recognizing our flaws in gentle and compassionate ways can bind us closer to others.

We must have patience with the unfolding of our lives and the world. God's kingdom unfolds in God's own time. We discover that we are not solely responsible for saving the world. Acknowledging our limits can liberate us from our compulsions and frantic busyness and lead us toward recognizing our interdependence. Each of our gifts contributes to the whole.

Meditation: Embodied Lectio Divina

You can practice lectio divina with your body as a sacred text.

Settling and Shimmering

Allow some time to settle in to your chair and sink into your body. Become aware of your breathing, gently deepening it. As you inhale, imagine the breath of God filling not just your body but also the whole of your life with enlivening energy. As you exhale, imagine letting go of whatever keeps you from being fully present to life.

Allow your breath to carry your awareness down to your heart center. Rest in this space for a few moments, perhaps resting your hand on your heart and relishing the rhythm of your heartbeat, which sustains your life.

Savoring and Stirring

Begin to "read" your experience. Scan through your body, beginning with your feet and slowly moving your awareness through your legs, hips, groin, back, stomach, shoulders, arms, neck, head, and face. Notice if there is one place in your body needing more attention. Be present to this place, bringing your breath there, softening into it, and opening to memories and feelings.

Listen for how your heart is being led. Make room within you to allow this place in your body to spark memories and feelings. Are there images, colors, or symbols rising up into your awareness? Be present to the feelings that are being stirred, and welcome them in.

Summoning and Serving

Begin to shift your awareness, and open to the ways God is present to you in this place in your body. Is there a sense of how you are being called in your life to respond to this moment? What action or awareness is emerging from your reflection on your body?

Slowing and Stilling

Gently release everything that has been stirring in you. Connect to your breath again, and allow the rhythm of your breath to fill you with peace as you let go of words and images so you can rest fully into a few moments of contemplative presence. Give yourself some time to simply be, remembering that your life is about more than the sum of your experiences and what you do in the world. Then release even this awareness and come to a place of deep stillness.

When you are ready to complete this time of prayer, allow your breath to gently bring your awareness back to your room. Take some time to journal about what emerged in your prayer experience, writing about the moment that called for more attention.

Creative Exploration: Trace Your Body Outline

Your invitation for a visual art experience is to trace a part of your body onto paper. You might want to seek out some large pieces of butcher paper from an arts-and-crafts store.

I recommend experimenting with your hand, but you can use any body part that is traceable. Let this outline be the container for a collage. Before you begin with images, spend a few moments listening to that part of yourself, holding the intention to tell the story of that part through found images. Then let the intention go as you enter the process. Let images choose you that both resonate and have a sense of dissonance. Glue them down as feels satisfying.

When you are done, spend some time in silence with your collage. Then let different images speak through journal writing. Enter into conversation with them. What story do they want to tell you? How does this part of your body long for the connection to joy? What is the grief being held?

For a larger exploration, purchase a bigger piece of butcher paper and ask a trusted friend to trace your body onto the paper. Then you can use paint, drawing materials, or collage to illuminate yourself.

Responses to the Embodied Lectio Divina

> I love, my body:
> gentle yet strong.
> Face and smile of softness
> I have often been told,
> and a strength that is rock solid!
> I say "yes" to that!
> I have been unfair to you so often
> pushed you beyond
> your limits—worked so hard
> to be for so many.
> Now, is your moment to be
> nurtured and cradled
> like a little baby,

ever watchful of your needs;
responding and respecting
every longing and feeling.

—Mary Lee

Haikus for My Body

with great tenderness
I touch the sacred within
this body of mine

stories of the past
I carried in every cell
are leaving me now

thirsty for new life
like tiny birds, beaks agape,
my cells drink nectar

this is my story
I create new beginnings
out of sad endings

—Deirdre McKeown

Honoring Breasts

Nourishing
and comforting

Others and our own

How
many do we hold upon our breasts

Their tears flow over them and through
   us like streams in
the spring

Nourishing
and comforting

We take them in with our eyes, small
   glimpses

Soothing
our inner child

They are there in the forefront like soft
   armor

Ready
to receive love and loss

In aging are they soft and supple?

Still
able to absorb the world

Women cradle the world in their breasts

Allowing
the life of others to pour into them

Flowing milk of God's love

Round
softness to lessen the hardness of our
        broken edges

—Pamela Phiefer Mathews

Movement Exploration

Yin Yoga: Reclining Twist

I invite you to try a reclining twist. You might bring an intention to this pose connected to our theme of incarnation. Perhaps you simply say to yourself that you will open to any grief residing in your body this day. Perhaps there is another intention you would like to hold.

Beginning on your back, have a timer with a gentle ring nearby set for three minutes so you do not have to watch the clock and can let yourself sink into the pose. Let your legs extend. Then bend both knees and bring your right leg over your left leg and let your lower body roll over to the ground to the left side. Your arms can be in a T-shape, and to deepen the stretch, turn your head to face the right. When you come into the twist, remember to focus on your breath. If your breathing is labored, you are in too far. If you are in any pain at all, come out.

Begin by bringing your breath to any places in your body that feel tight, and let them soften with each exhale. As you stay in the pose, places of holding and tightness may emerge over time, so as you become aware of this, keep bringing the breath to your body. Let your awareness sink down into your muscles and tendons. Let this practice be a time of intimacy with your body, experiencing it from within.

As thoughts arise, whether boredom, anxiety, or judgment, imagine softening them with the breath, and then let them go with each exhale. As waves of emotion come through your body, soften your heart and let them move through you. If no particular feeling arises, you don't have to manufacture or force this; just simply let it be as it is.

When the timer rings, bring your body back to center again; rock gently to release your spine, and then come into the pose on the other side.

Mudras: Embodying Qualities with Your Hands

In the Buddhist and Hindu traditions we find many *mudras*, a Sanskrit word meaning "gesture." Mudras are hand gestures that symbolize different qualities and evoke different energetic responses within the body. There are mudras for compassion, for courage, for equanimity, and so forth. You may be familiar with the traditional prayer position of palms touching each other and placed in front of the heart with a bow at the end of a yoga class. Often the word *namaste* is uttered, which means "may the divine in me greet the divine in you."

There is a similar tradition in Christianity. The figures in Eastern Orthodox icons often are depicted with hands or fingers in certain positions as an act of blessing. Hands outstretched to receive Communion is a common practice on most Sundays in churches. Sometimes when we pray, we clasp our hands together in a prayer position, a way of embodying our heart's longings. These are all ways we have expressed the incarnation of our prayers in a physical way.

St. Dominic, a twelfth- to thirteenth-century Spanish priest and founder of the Dominican order, had several ways of praying with the body, including hand gestures to express specific qualities. He is known for nine ways in particular.[4] For your movement practice, I invite you first to explore some of these more traditional hand and arm postures from St. Dominic:

Orans: Begin by choosing some music and stand tall, feet slightly apart. Stretch your arms outward, reaching to each side. This is known as the Orans and is a posture of supplication, taking the shape of the cross with your body. Experiment with this posture through dance, exploring how you might move through space with your arms outstretched. Perhaps you raise your arms with palms up. You can bring your elbows closer into your body. Play around with it through movement, and see what you discover. Allow a few minutes to let this dance unfold.

Stretching Heavenward: This is another body prayer form Dominic describes in which both your arms are raised overhead and your hands clasped together. In this way, your body forms a kind of arrow pointed heavenward. You might play with feeling your energy move from the earth beneath you through your body and then skyward and then back down again. Bring this into your dance. Play with releasing your hands but still directing them upward. See where the dance leads.

Palms Cupped: Extend your hands out in front of you, forming a bowl shape with your palms facing upward. Let this be the starting place for your dance, and move through space exploring variations on this position of receiving.

When we embody these postures, we incarnate certain qualities and connect to an ancient tradition and practice of praying in this way. After experimenting with these more traditional prayers of supplication, extending, and receiving, put on a new piece of music and allow a few moments to be still and tune in with your body. Allow your body to create its own mudra or posture. Play with it, dance with it in different variations, and then listen for what quality it seems to embody for you. Or you might begin by contemplating a quality you want to bring into your life and then finding a posture or gesture that expresses this for you. See if this might be a mudra prayer you can bring into your dance and movement practice in a regular way to play with incarnating this way of being in your life.

Reflection Questions

- How does embracing the truth of the incarnation call you to live in your own holy body?
- What does it mean for you to trust your body? How does this look in practical ways?
- When you remember your earthiness, what images are evoked?

Closing Blessing

Body Psalm for
Remembering Back Your Passion

Remember back the body
flames in the belly
calling one to live
as each day is the first and the last
Your life is a precious
entity of cells and blood
quirks and sentences of glory

Remember back the passion
don't let the awe
slip from your fingers
toes, hips, pelvis and voice
Draw back into presence your own calling
for what you are meant to do and be
on this glorious planet
coupled with the paradox of terror and beauty

It is not only the earth
which needs greening
but your own precious soul
sometimes lost in the meetings, emails, or laundry.

Remember back all of you
messy and unpredictable
veins pulsing with a hopefulness
to thirst for more.
Hunger is your spiritual director
Coming in all forms—
discontent or agitation

Press on to what is nudging you
breathing you back into
inhabiting your own body

The calling of your life
lies at the door
waiting for you.

—Celeste Snowber

Chapter 8

Ecstasy and Reclaiming Joy: Expanding Our Threshold of Tolerance

Come, dervishes: here is the water of life. Dance in it.

—Thomas Merton

In 2011 I traveled to Santa Fe, New Mexico, for a BodySoul Rhythms workshop led by Sherry Wheaton and Linda Kawer. BodySoul Rhythms is a powerful embodied practice founded by Jungian analyst Marion Woodman. Wheaton introduced the program with an image that has been incredibly helpful for me both personally and in my own teaching.

She described how we each have a threshold of tolerance in our lives where we feel at ease in the world, calm and centered. Beyond this, when life offers us stressful circumstances and the changes that will inevitably come, we move either in the direction of anxiety or numbness. Sometimes we move through anxiety to numbness or vice versa, but we often have a dominant pattern for coping.

If we consciously practice dancing at the edges of our threshold of tolerance by intentionally putting ourselves into situations that will make us uncomfortable—perhaps a dance workshop or yoga class, or maybe an art or writing experience—but we are able to back off whenever necessary, we can actually begin to expand our threshold of tolerance by mindfully widening the edges. We stay grounded by tending to our breath and tracking our inner experience. We step toward what frightens us within a safe and supportive environment, and then we have the chance to practice new ways of responding to discomfort and challenge.

When our threshold expands, we become more resilient, less anxious and numb, and more capable of experiencing the deep well of emotion in life. It has been my distinct experience that our capacity for joy is in direct proportion to our capacity for grief. The more we do the honest work of allowing our emotions free movement within us, the greater the possibility that joy will be one of those feelings that comes to visit or reside in us.

After years of deep grief over the death of my mother, a grief that at times I thought might never lighten, I have moved to a place in my life where I also experience the most exquisite kind of joy. Much of this joy has broken free for me through the practice of dance. Often when I begin dancing tears rise up, first tears of grief that I may not even know the origin of, which is okay. Then comes space for this incredible sense of bliss to expand within me. Not all the time does this happen, and not every time, but often enough that I trust the dance to connect me to that soul-expanding place. It is an embodied experience, not a joy created by my thoughts but a full-bodied delight experienced through my senses, intuition, and body sensation. In the process of learning to trust the grief, I have also come to trust the joy, and I find myself relishing the sweetness of each.

The Call of Ecstasy

> *Ekstasis*—to stand outside of oneself, to be drawn beyond oneself into some larger reality. . . . In the early Christian monastic tradition, John Cassian used the phrase *excessus mentis* (evoking the feeling of being drawn beyond or outside the boundaries of one's mind) to express that particular sense of overflowing that often accompanies intense spiritual experience, the strange

sensation of being taken out of oneself, of floating in an
endless expanse.

—Douglas Christie, *The Blue Sapphire of the Mind*

Ecstasy may call to mind strange images of illegal drugs or someone out
of control with emotion or rapture. In fact, ecstasy was often experienced by many of the Christian mystics, and it is our natural birthright. I
believe it has been dismissed by many religious institutions because it is
not an experience that can be controlled. The very nature of ecstasy is to
lose control, to move past your own boundaries and experience a sense
of union with creation, with God, or with another human being.

Reflect for a moment on your own experiences of ecstasy. Perhaps
they came while standing in a pine forest or on the peak of a mountain,
maybe it was the moment of orgasm or in holding a beloved in sweet
rest, your limbs tangled with one another. Maybe you have tasted ecstasy
in beholding an infant—your own, a grandchild, or the child of another—and you suddenly knew yourself connected, no longer separate. Or
perhaps it was in releasing yourself to the sometimes-exquisite freedom
of dance and realizing for a moment that there was no self-consciousness, that you were simply creation itself dancing. The soft animal of
your body got lost in the music and sense of connection. Or it is possible you don't have any memory of ecstatic moments and maybe a grief
rises up. Whatever your experience, bring compassion and curiosity to
yourself.

When we hold back from being in our bodies, we hold back from the
possibility of ecstatic moments. Ecstasy is embodied; it is not something
we think our way through, as it demands a surrender that only the body
in union with the soul can offer.

You might remember the Song of Songs as a favorite text of mystics and monks precisely because its highly charged erotic language was
symbolic of the experience of an encounter with the Divine. It evoked
this same sense of loss of boundaries and forgetting oneself.

The mystical tradition is clear that the state of ecstasy—when the
human person is caught up into union with the Divine—is considered

highly favorable. Jungian analyst Robert A. Johnson wrote a book about ecstasy, describing it as the psychology of joy.[1] The word has become synonymous with joyous exaltation, and yet we might often find ourselves holding back. Much like the emotions of grief or anger, sometimes joy is just as difficult because there is a sense of moving beyond oneself and losing some control, of giving yourself over to the joy that you resist.

One of the profound things I have discovered after years of being on a descent and dark-night experience is that the depth of my commitment to staying present to my grief and lament has also revealed an unspeakable height of joy on the other side.

Our sexuality and spirituality both arise from the same longing: from our desire for connection to another, whether a friend, partner, lover, or the Divine. They press us against our vulnerability because we discover that we can't go through this life alone. We have to risk betrayal and wounding, and so this path of intimacy and prayer is fraught with fear of losing control. We then resist the ecstasy and also lose touch with the capacity for joy.

Dancing Our Deepest Joy

> What is serious to men and women is often very trivial in the sight of God. What in God might appear to us as "play" is perhaps what he himself takes most seriously. At any rate the Lord plays and diverts himself in the garden of his creation, and if we could let go of our own obsession with what we think is the meaning of it all, we might be able to hear his call and follow him in his mysterious, cosmic dance. . . . Yet the fact remains that we are invited to forget ourselves on purpose, cast our awful solemnity to the winds and join in the general dance.
>
> —Thomas Merton, *New Seeds of Contemplation*

Dance is a celebration of the life force at work within us. When we step into the dance as prayer, we may find ourselves connecting to this great cosmic dance of which Merton writes. We may feel joy, pleasure, hope, beauty, and playfulness. Grief may arrive as well. Dance can thrust us quickly to the edges of our discomfort.

It was in that workshop in Santa Fe where I reclaimed my inner dancer at the age of forty. I had just the previous Christmas been through the frightening experience with a pulmonary embolism I described in chapter 3. I was feeling vulnerable and extraordinarily grateful for life, but I was also aware that my life was limited and there were things I wanted to no longer postpone.

In one of the movement meditations, we were invited to look into the closets of our psyches and invite out whatever might be hiding there. For me it was my dancer. I had danced in different ways in the years prior, but in that moment, I connected to this part of myself in a deeper way. I claimed her as a sacred part of who I am. I claimed her as a threshold to more joyful, expressive, and embodied living.

I love so much that Thomas Merton ends *New Seeds of Contemplation*, one of my favorite books of his, with this exquisite quotation about the cosmic dance. There is so much that weighs us down daily. What would it mean to consider taking ourselves less seriously and respond to this invitation to dance?

The most direct path to ecstasy is dance. Dance for me is both a literal reality and a metaphorical one. When we dance through life, we take things more lightly; we allow the river of grief to flow through us, and we yield our bodies and hearts to it. We dance in daily life by moving slowly and with intention, by responding with flexibility and grace, and by not letting our fear of what others think keep us from expressing our heart's deep desires.

This is the doorway to transformation. The universe is already dancing; we are just called to say yes and stop fighting it so much. Ecstasy brings us to an awareness of something beyond ourselves. When we learn to love our bodies, this ease and joy overflows into our relationships, and we give witness to a different way of being in the world. We discover new intimacy with creation because we recognize ourselves as creatures with an animal nature. We grow closer to God because we have finally let go of that last barricade, the subtle feeling that our bodies are somehow deficient rather than the exquisite gifts they are.

Ally on the Journey: St. Teresa of Avila

> I saw in his hand a long spear of gold, and at the iron's point there seemed to be a little fire. He appeared to me to be thrusting it at times into my heart, and to pierce my very entrails; when he drew it out, he seemed to draw them out also, and to leave me all on fire with a great love of God. The pain was so great, that it made me moan; and yet so surpassing was the sweetness of this excessive pain, that I could not wish to be rid of it. The soul is satisfied now with nothing less than God. The pain is not bodily, but spiritual; though the body has its share in it. It is a caressing of love so sweet which now takes place between the soul and God, that I pray God of his goodness to make him experience it who may think that I am lying.
>
> —Teresa of Avila, *The Life of St. Teresa of Jesus*

St. Teresa of Avila, depicted in the famous sculpture by Bernini in Rome in the fullness of her ecstatic moment, is another companion to join our holy caravan. In this statue we see her depicted in the midst of mystical ecstasy and the fervor of her love for God. You can almost see on her face the way she has transcended herself and embraced a much wider reality.

She is clothed in a long, loose garment with bare feet. Her left foot is revealed, her eyes are shut, and her mouth is open in a posture of swooning. The angel beside her points an arrow toward her heart. The statue depicts Teresa's own description of her experience written about in chapter 29 of *The Life of St. Teresa of Jesus*. She is in the throes of delight, and rather than downplaying it, the statue celebrates it.

Invite her presence in as a wise guide into the path of ecstasy. Ask Teresa to show you the joy that is your birthright and to support you in releasing whatever stands in the pathway to this deep, abiding joyfulness.

Practice: Gratitude

> Gratitude is the basis for ecstasy, the state of consciousness in which we fully embrace whatever we are experiencing.
>
> —Bill Pfeiffer, *Wild Earth, Wild Soul*

In Benedict's Rule he counsels and encourages an attitude of contentment among the monks. Whatever the circumstances they find themselves in, they are to find some satisfaction with what is in the moment. In a world of self-entitlement and inflated sense of need, learning to be content with what we have has the potential to be quite revolutionary. It means craving less and being more satisfied with what one has.

One way to practice this posture of contentment is gratitude. Gratitude is a way of being in the world that does not assume we are owed anything, and the fact that we have something at all—whether our lives, our breath, families, friends, shelter, laughter, or other simple pleasures—is cause for celebration. We can cultivate a way of being in the world that treats all these things as gifts, knowing none of us deserve particular graces.

We can begin with gratitude for the most basic of gifts: life itself. Let's wake each morning for another day to live and love, grateful for our breath and a body that allows us to move through our day. Then we can offer gratitude for a home and all the things that are important to us about home. Gratitude is a practice that can begin with the smallest acknowledgment and be expanded out to every facet of our existence. A simple way to nurture this awareness in our lives is to end each day with a gratitude list. You can either write five to ten things in your journal for which you feel grateful that day or set a timer for one or two minutes and write down everything that comes to mind. It is a way to end the day by honoring the gifts we have received rather than dwelling on where life came up short for us.

Another possibility for practice is to write a thank-you letter to someone from your life who touched you in a particular way. It could be a grade-school teacher who always made you feel supported or a clerk at the library who went out of his way to get you something you needed for a research paper. Our lives are continually intersecting with others who extend themselves in quiet ways to help us.

Gratitude has a way of transforming our approach to life into one that is more open-hearted, generous, and joyful. Rather than moving through our day feeling cynical or burdened, we can consciously choose our thoughts. This doesn't mean we have to offer gratitude for injustices or abuse; we are always called to resist those. But it does mean we might be able to tap into greater joy to replenish us for those moments when we need to fight for dignity and kindness. Gratitude overflows into joy and makes us feel connected to something bigger than ourselves.

Meditation: Mirror Prayer

For instance, I can say that I think it is important to pray naked in front of a full-length mirror sometimes, especially when you are full of loathing for your body. Maybe you think you are too heavy. Maybe you have never liked the way your hip bones stick out. Do your breasts sag? Are you too hairy? It is always something. . . .

You have gotten glimpses of your body as you have bathed or changed clothes, but so far maintaining your equilibrium has depended upon staying covered up as much as you can. You have even discovered how to shower in the dark so that you may have to feel what you presently loathe about yourself but you do not have to look at it.

This can only go on so long, especially for someone who officially believes that God loves flesh and blood, no matter what kind of shape it is in. Whether you are sick or well, lovely or irregular, there comes a time when it is vitally important for your spiritual health to drop your clothes, look in the mirror, and say, "Here I am. This is the body-like-no-other that my life has shaped. I live here. This is my soul's address."

—Barbara Brown Taylor, *An Altar in the World*

I invite you into a mirror prayer with your body. Notice your first and instinctive response to these words. Notice if the thought fills you with fear, loathing, or reticence, and bring compassion to yourself. Or maybe you find the whole idea of looking at yourself as too filled with vanity. Or perhaps there is a sense of anticipation at what you might discover after having made the journey so far. Welcome whatever your experience is without judgment. This experience isn't about trying to feel a particular way but about noticing and discovering what is true for you right now and holding that with love and compassion.

Find a private place. Breathe gently, slowing yourself down. Begin with a prayer for God to help you to see yourself as fully whole and beautiful and created in love. Begin by remembering that you have the strength to see yourself as you are and to tame back those critical thoughts. When they arise, return to your breath. When we are aware of the breath, our minds have something to focus on so they can release their relentless narrative for a time.

When you feel ready, or at least when you have summoned the courage to step past your resistance, disrobe and allow yourself time in front of a mirror to simply gaze with love on yourself. When the loving thoughts evaporate, return to them again and again.

Bring both curiosity and reverence to the folds of skin, the sags, the wrinkles and dimples, and the stretch marks and scars. For now, just notice if there is a story that arises that could bring a sense of honoring to your embodied self. Perhaps it is seeing stretch marks and the memory of giving birth to your children. Maybe it is the years of experience those furrows reveal or the warrior's pride in her scars. Or maybe there is more lament arising: grief or anger at all the ways you have showed your physical self disdain and all the ways you have depleted yourself to please others. Let your experience unfold, trusting your body as much as you can. And then remember how extraordinarily resilient the body is. Remember the years of trials and joys you have traveled with this, your soul's address.

Imagine what it would be like to gaze upon your body and see it for the sanctuary it is. Imagine arriving in a place where the self-scrutiny and criticism shed away like old skin, revealing something renewed beneath, a sense of being at home.

What if your gratitude practice could extend to this beautiful body you live in? Imagine saying thank you to each and every part for doing the best they could. And if this still feels very far away, keep returning to compassion; keep returning to a gaze of love.

Responses to the Mirror Prayer

Gazing in the mirror
I see beautiful
strong yet gentle
and pensive you

I want to hug you
stroke your hair
rub your shoulders
hold your hands

Do not think too much
about yesterdays
of things not done well
or things not done at all

As a gardener you know
there is a time for everything
a time for working but also
a time to just let things happen

What is it you need
in order to live
in a way
that nourishes you?

Always be grateful
for this body

how it has carried you
held you safely

Honor it daily
feasting
on all the greenness
as well as the bareness

Continue to light candles in prayer
read, write, plant seeds
explore and be with nature
But, don't forget to dance!

—Eve Marrero Davila

I stand in front of the mirror and gaze at the body before me—aged—like fine wine—aged—like stinky cheese—aged and beautiful.

I stand before the mirror and I see me—warped, dull, glowing. I live here. This is my soul's address and that address, I have not lost.

I live here now. Today. This moment. Enough for a day. A lifetime. A lifeline. This is my soul's address 91156 NW Kayce Road.

The road traveled has been mine. It is me. I live here. I have not lost this address even though storms have threatened to sweep my road away. I live here in simplicity and magnificence—in achy bones and stiff muscles—in fluid dancer's body and yogic poses. I live here. This is my soul's address. And that address, I have not lost.

—Kayce Stevens Hughlett

Creative Exploration: Poem of Instruction

I invite you to write a poem of instruction. This is a form of poetry offering advice on how to do something. For this chapter, my suggestion would be something like "How to Embrace Your Joy" or "How to Live Joyfully in a Body."

Begin by free writing everything that comes to mind. Imagine you are writing advice to someone younger, perhaps even your own younger self. Allow ten minutes of writing down everything that comes to mind without editing. Then go through and delete extraneous words or phrases.

You may just have a list already that works as a poem. Post it somewhere as a reminder to yourself.

Responses to the Poem of Instruction

open the soft mouth of your heart,
this is the start,
where your story begins

underneath layers of
achievements, errands, demands,
cravings, compulsions, criticisms,
there is—buried deep—a seed,
there is—far below—a hunger

you are quietly waiting to grow
you are far more hungry than you know

so feed that little seed
with Water, Sun, and Spirit
hold it in the soft Earth of your soul
let its roots sink deep and deeper still
feel it spread through you
with its soft tendrils
let it find and form
in every crevice of who you are

then, let it sprout!
let it grow out of the top of your head
let the seed become a sapling,
then, let it become a tree

let your tree grow
let its arms unfurl to kiss the sky
and hold the sun
and dance in the rain
and bow to the wind
let it grow!

let the clouds form a crown for you, set
        with stars
let birds and squirrels dwell in your
        branches
with their song and their scurry
let the leaves of your spring and summer
go in your fall
and then wait in your winter,
hopeful in rest

be this tree
that reaches up and reaches down
whose profound hunger for Life
makes it grow, strong and tall
whose gentle submission to Life
makes it stand, wise and patient
be the tree
whose roots run through you
whose trunk shoots forth
from the crown of your head
be the tree

start by opening
the soft mouth of your heart

—Stephanie Warner Jenkins

Eat green foods
Drink fresh water
Repeat as often as possible,
As a daily prayer.
Ask for God's help
Call upon the earth's healing energy
Repeat as often as possible,
As a daily prayer
Laugh heartily from the belly
Move the body with joy
Repeat as often as possible,
As a daily prayer.
Breathe deeply and fully
Connect with kindred spirits, or the
    silence
Repeat as often as possible,
As a daily prayer.
Know that if you are ever too busy
To take part in these daily sacraments
Then you are too busy . . .
Ask yourself—what keeps me from
eating green foods
drinking fresh water
asking for God's help
calling upon the earth's healing energy
laughing heartily from the belly
moving with joy
breathing deeply and fully
connecting with kindred spirits or
    silence . . .

Listen to your breath, listen to your
    body—
The answer will arrive.

                     —Jamie Marich

Corporeal Welcome

I see you.
I honor you.
Fleshing of my spirit,
namaste.

You are a living story,
a testimony to resilience,
a topographical map tracing my history,
a reminder that life is more
than the chaos erupting in my thoughts.

Through your trembling, tremoring
    muscles,
the bruises that bloom with each
    mis-step,
the pared down food that you require,
you slow down
the ever-accelerating lists of tasks
yet to be complete.

Help me remember
you are a holy space,
each inhale and exhale
a bellows igniting spirit in me.

Root me in earth
Ground me in faith

Bathe me in gratitude
Anoint me with hope
Help me be present to myself.

Let me live in possibility:
Open Mind
Open Heart
Open Will

—Lisa Murray

I gaze into the mirror,
hair uncombed
sigh!
It's been a long road.
the body
no longer symmetrical
scarred, saggy
obese
I LOVE IT
IT IS MINE
I know its history
intimately
I know the story
of every dimple
and pimple
of every torn muscle
and bruise;
an outside image
of the inside cruise.

My body
has served me well
no longer about survival
I need more, I smile

I need to love it and honor it
celebrate the one who has been with me
every step of the way.
I take out my oil made with Labrador tea,
bless the oil, and with the oil bless me.
each chakra,
each limb and joint
the feet
which have carried me this far
the hands
that interact with everyone
and everything
my eyes, nose and ears
the mouth, that smiles
when words don't do justice
my rectum and private parts
all the associated fluids and noise
my breasts,
which once attracted attention
and suckled my children
and are now competing with my navel
for a place to rest.
I was at first shy to look
to approach the mirror
with the intent to dwell
and really see.
I shrugged off the guilt,
and opened my eyes
at how much I have abused,
hidden and believed the lies.
I would not have treated
any other human being this way
Can I learn to respect and trust
this beauty before me?

Can I befriend the one
that has been with me
all along?

—Camilla Caughlin

Movement Exploration

Yin Yoga: Happy Baby

In happy baby pose, lie down on your back, bend your knees toward your chest, and then grab either your feet, your calves, or the backs of your thighs, gently pulling your knees down and apart. You should feel a stretch in the hip and groin area. You can then rock back and forth like a happy baby if that feels good in your body.

This is a very vulnerable pose, which can be part of its beauty. Be mindful for yourself if it feels too vulnerable for you right now. When you come into it, know that you can release at any time you need to. You could also choose to move into *savasana* (corpse or resting pose) or child's pose instead.

Settle into stillness, breathing slowly and deeply. Notice where you feel the stretch. Become aware of thoughts that feel tight or restricting, and bring your breath to your mind to gently soften them. Consciously invite a sense of bliss and joy into your pose. Smile inwardly, and become aware of anything in your life that evokes gratitude. Bask in these grateful feelings for the rest of your pose.

When you are done, gently release your legs and spend a few moments in the full relaxation of corpse pose, allowing the previous pose to integrate into your body.

Body Blessing Dance

Blessing is an act of gratitude for the gifts we have been given. This act of blessing is really a special way of paying attention. It is a moment of remembering wonder as our primary response to the world. It is an act of consecrating whatever it is we are noticing.

Find some music that inspires you to dance. Prepare yourself for moving inward by tending to your breath and to your heart. Put your hands over your heart and give thanks for the wonder of this blood that pumps through your body; give thanks for the breath that infuses you. Take a moment to honor these automatic rhythms that sustain life. Bless your breath and heartbeat.

As the music begins, allow your body to move as it wants to. There's no need to control this dance. Gently bring your awareness to each part of your body in the list. As you move to each new place in your body, begin by blessing it and offering gratitude for all the ways it has served you in this life. As you dance, hold the following questions lightly and see how your body responds.

Feet: How do you walk in the world? Offer gratitude for the gift of feet and the places they have taken you.

Legs: How do you stand in the world? What journeys have your legs carried you on? Offer gratitude for the gift of legs and how they have helped you to stand and journey forth.

Pelvis: What have you given birth to in the world? Which dreams and visions have come to reality through you? Offer gratitude for the gift of your hips and how they nourish your creative visions.

Belly: What nourishes you most? How have you been well nourished? Offer gratitude for the gift of your belly and how it helps you take in life-giving food.

Chest and Heart: Whom have you loved? Offer gratitude for the gift of your heart and how it has inspired passion and intimacy in your life.

Back: What are you carrying? What burdens have you borne on your back that you set aside? Offer gratitude for the gift of your back and all that it has allowed you to carry.

Arms: How have your arms enabled you to embrace life and those you love? Offer gratitude for the gift of your arms and all those you have wrapped them around.

Throat: How has your throat allowed you to speak or sing your truth in the world? Offer gratitude for the gift of your neck and throat and how it facilitates your voice.

Face: What is the face you show to the world? Offer gratitude for the gift of your face and what you reveal to others.

After blessing each part, bring your awareness back to the whole of your body and bless your whole being. Rest in stillness for a few moments before reflecting on the experience in writing.

Reflection Questions

- What are you discovering about your own openness and resistance to ecstasy in your life?
- How might you make a daily practice of cultivating gratitude?
- How might the mirror become a friend and ally in the journey toward body celebration?

Closing Blessing

Body Psalm for Raw Joy

Don't look for Easter outside you
it is within you

the outrageous birth of new life
is inside, under the ground
erupting through your body
enlivening your tissues
Resurrection is not a restricted zone
it is the lungs of your life
you are birthed anew each day
Easter celebrates the resurrection of Christ
this is not a one-time event
but breathes inside you each moment
spring asks
to look within and
pay attention to Spirit
Look at the faithfulness of new growth
even in the midst of a world
aching with troubles and tribulations
ecological cries and the haunts of war
the plants and trees still bud
the call to new life
p e r s i s t s
You live in a riparian zone
between the worlds
of earth and heaven
the gift of life in this body
beckons you to
an easter life
where you feed
on raw joy.

—Celeste Snowber

Chapter 9

The Greening of the Body: The Earth As Matrix

Take earth for your own large room
and the floor of earth
carpeted with sunlight
and hung round with silver wind
for your dancing place.

—May Swenson, "Earth Your Dancing Place"

The earth is the great biosphere that sustains our life moment by moment, providing oxygen and nourishment to our bodies. Our bodies are essentially the animal aspect of ourselves, primal and full of the wisdom of instinct. Even though we may sometimes be tempted to view ourselves as separate from it—as objective observers rather than subjective participants—we are woven into this earth web.

The root of the word *matrix* comes from the Latin *mater*, which means "mother" or "womb." Like a womb, a matrix is a field out of which something emerges or is given birth to.

The earth is the very matrix—the origin and sustaining environment—out of which bodies emerge. The earth is the first place where we experience the kind of deep physical nourishment necessary for our beings to thrive, and it is also a place of symbolic experience where we begin to make meaning from our suffering. A matrix is a place of grounding and birthing.

When we pay attention to the rhythms of the rise and fall of each day and the seasons, when we tend to the power of migration, and when we see all of the cycles and processes of the natural world as windows into understanding not just our bodies but our souls as well, we have access to an immense and ancient source of wisdom.

Your Body's Wild Calling

It is the time of the great migrations; wild winged ones fly in ragged formations away from the summer fields of plenty, down from the tundra, up from the tropics, ordinary hearts beating against the winds, resisting the updrafts, into the storms, through the autumnal fogs that hide the hunters and the seductions of rest; wild finned ones turn against the familiar ocean currents to slip through narrow stony channels, leaping against the steepness of the grade, following an ancient invocation of leave and return. Fin and feather, flesh, blood and bone: the earth calls its creatures to leave the familiar, turn again into the unknown; to move steadily and continuously and at great risk toward an invisible goal, expending great energy with the possibility of failure; to live on migratory pathways into the future; the primal logic of survival and regeneration, an ancient summons, nature's pull against the grain, against all odds, against the reasonable and the safe; reconstituting the world.

—Marianne Worcester

As I read this quote and open myself body and soul to it, I can feel a yearning in my physical self. I can imagine the ancient call and longing that guides the wild winged ones to discover the places luring their great beating hearts forward.

Consider Worcester's words and what the natural patterns of migration evoke in us: leaving the familiar and moving toward what is unknown; growing toward an invisible longing; risking failure in service of a call; and rejecting the safe path in favor of something more tenuous and ultimately more alive and generative. In just that one simple paragraph, what from those ideas calls to your own deep being? How do the ancient migratory patterns that call the swans, salmon, and whales across vast landscapes live in your own beating heart? Have you felt the great aliveness that comes from following an invisible thread somewhere beyond the horizon of your own imagining?

Pause for a moment and breathe into your heart; let your animal body experience the desires that call it forward. What do you notice? What do you hear?

As we come to know the ancient patterns and ways of creation, we come to know ourselves. We want to reject the false distinction between ourselves and the rest of nature. We seek instead to remember with our whole bodies the ancient rhythms that still pulse through us.

Wildness is that which cannot be tamed. We try so hard to domesticate our lives, the world around us, God, and perhaps most of all, our bodies. Yet wildness continues to call to us, to reject those places where we have narrowed our lives and refused to consider that more expansiveness awaits us than we can imagine. Wildness says you do not need to fit into the narrowly defined image others think is acceptable. The ways you hold your body back for fear of judgment also has an impact on your soul. The creatures of this earth never think, *I will make this journey of the heart once I lose twenty pounds.* Birds, fish, and animals live from their bodily nature and instinct and remind us we have that same wisdom available to us.

A few years ago I was teaching one of our "Awakening the Creative Spirit" five-day intensives for spiritual directors. It was the middle of the week in the afternoon, and I was feeling tired. My teaching partner, Betsey, was leading us in movement that day, and I was feeling some fatigue and internal resistance. It was a glorious spring day outside, so we went out onto the lawn in front of the retreat center. There we spent some time just lying in the grass, connecting to our bodies, rolling around, and paying attention to what would feel good and nourishing.

After about ten minutes of letting myself go and allowing the grass to support me, I discovered that my energy had completely shifted. I felt this surge of aliveness, of newness, and of vitality. My body was awakened by this earth connection. I later discovered that the reiki tradition has a similar practice called "earthing," which is a way of honoring the earth's—its grass, dirt, stone, sand, and more—natural healing and subtle energies that we can draw upon for our own healing and rejuvenation.

When we adopted our previous dog, Winter, we quickly discovered that one of her favorite spiritual practices was "rolling in the grass meditation." Once spring arrived and the ground was no longer cold and wet, I found myself drawn to join her. I suddenly remembered my experience at the retreat and wondered if that could happen again; indeed it did, over and over.

When I am feeling tired, a walk does wonders. When I feel really depleted and even a walk feels too draining, lying down in the grass, smelling the earth, and feeling the dew against my skin never fails to revive me. I am sure there is some scientific explanation for all of this—maybe it has to do with negative ions or some such thing—but all I know is that it works. And I think the implications are huge. Nature restores us so immediately when we allow ourselves to get down on the ground and roll around. We return to our bodies as the locus of awareness and knowing. We give our bodies the gift of restoration at the source.

Ask yourself again if you are willing to make the descent into the wilderness of the body. Remembering your animal senses, your own inherent wildness can be frightening because it means opening yourself to that wilder, wider horizon of possibility, the one that stretches far beyond our own limited imaginations. It is a much more humble place to live in, one where we are never certain of anything anymore. Except, perhaps, once we have access to this place within us, it is very difficult, if not impossible, to return to a fully domesticated consciousness. We are no longer satisfied holding back under the judgment that our bodies are not good enough or thin enough or feel well enough. Our bodies long for this journey just as they are.

Reclaiming our wild natures is the only way to remember who we truly are and discover what earth-rattling calling really awaits us outside of the safe confines of our daily lives. Does this make you tremble just a little? It should. Approaching the holy in its wild guise has always evoked quaking and commotion in human hearts, precisely because this force is so beyond our boxes. We will not fix or control the earth with our rational, logical analyses. Science is essential to our understanding, but it must be married with soulful wisdom about how to actually live.

When we respond to the wild call to adventure, it is always beyond the confines of ego and culture, even beyond the guarantees of certainty and survival. We know nature can be fierce and relentless in addition to being sublime and beautiful. There are no guarantees, which is why the journey is so frightening. Yet the alternative is to stay domesticated and tame, obeying rules and conventions, holding back, and coming to the end of our lives wondering if our bodies were just a waiting zone or whether they could have been a wild zone of awakening.

Our psyches are embedded in the life of our bodies. The body is our most immediate home on earth where all of our stories, joys, fears, and hopes are sculpted into flesh and muscle. The body is also the guardian of our insights and intuitions, of our deep yearnings and ripening, and of our celebration of life on earth. Our bodies are not separate from the earth but are inherently connected to the natural world: its minerals, air, and water are our bones, breath, and blood.

Seasons of the Earth, Seasons of Our Bodies

One of the great gifts of seasonal awareness for me has been an invitation to embrace all of the seasons within my own body.

Spring is a dynamic time of blossoming, when the world begins to break open through the splendor of color. These are the times my body awakens to new energy and aliveness.

Summer is a season of fruitfulness, when the earth's bounty comes to her fullness and we are well nourished. My body in summer energy feels at its height of passion and presence.

Autumn enters into the great release of the earth, harvesting the gifts and releasing what is not necessary. When my body is in its own autumn, it may feel more tired and in need of rest and of letting go of the long list of things to do.

Winter calls us into the grace of stillness and incubation, knowing the dark has her own wisdom that must be embraced before spring arrives again. My body in winter craves the restoration of deep sleep.

In our rushed and harried lives, we expect our bodies to stay perpetually in spring and summer cycles. We exhaust ourselves through our pace and expectations but are annoyed on days when we feel tired. Sometimes we fall ill because our bodies so desperately need rest, and it is only when we are ill that we give ourselves permission to stop. But then we can feel frustrated when we don't get better as quickly as we would like.

To remember the earth body is to embrace the fullness of her seasons in the world around us and within us. Perhaps we can grow gentler with ourselves when we remember that sometimes our bodies need to be in a period of autumn and winter release and restoration in order to summon the energy for spring again.

What are the rhythms that are most nourishing to you? Even if you have to work at a job during specific hours, is there one day per week when you can follow your own rhythms and tune in to what your body most deeply wants and needs?

Ally on the Journey: St. Brigid of Kildare

Christ dwells in every creature.

—Attributed to St. Brigid

We welcome another presence into our circle of allies for this journey, one who had a sense of hospitality and of the sacred dwelling in all things, which the quote above expresses. St. Brigid, also known as Mary of the Gaels, lived in the fifth and sixth centuries in Ireland and founded a monastery in Kildare, a name that means "church of the oak" and a town that was also the site of an earlier pagan shrine.

She is one of the three patron saints of Ireland and is wrapped in much legend and mystery. There was an earlier goddess in pre-Christian tradition named Brigid, and much of what we know about the saint also overlaps with the goddess, who was patron of poetry, smithwork, and healing.

Brigid's father was a chieftain; her mother was a slave baptized by St. Patrick. Her feast day is on February 1, which in the Celtic Wheel of the Year is also Imbolc and acts as essentially the very beginning of spring. The snowdrop—the first of spring's flowers—is one of her symbols, along with the white cow she had that was said to accompany her and provide milk for all who needed it.

Practice: Asceticism and the Call to Simplicity

Sadly much of the legacy of the ancient monks around the body has to do with extremes of fasting and self-denial. Asceticism is a way of denying oneself certain pleasures in the service of connecting to what feels most essential and important. While this can be a good practice, the shadow side of this occurs when we let the practice itself become the focus of our striving, when it becomes a kind of achievement or competition.

You may wonder what place asceticism has in our journey together of reclaiming our deep desires and the sensual pleasures of the body. Is there a place for stripping away those things we have been working so hard to reclaim?

This is the paradox of the spiritual life: holding everything in balance and recognizing the goodness of desire and pleasure, as well as the insight we gain when consciously withholding something we really long for to become more aware of what is most important.

There is something beautiful about reclaiming a healthy asceticism in our day. In a world where we consume far more resources than is sustainable for the earth, asceticism calls us back to remembering what we need for the sustainability of all. It reminds us of the gifts of simplicity and that our patterns of consumption in an effort to fill any emptiness within will always be futile.

If we can begin to look courageously and honestly at our own places where our egos grasp more than we need and listen to what our bodies most need, we may be able to see the disconnect between body and earth.

Meditation: Participation in the Life of Creation

When we allow ourselves to enter deeply and radically into the body of the earth and remember that our physical boundaries extend past the surface of our skin, we discover that we are intimately connected to all of creation. This is what I invite you to practice: a moment of sheer self-forgetting, a time of immersion in the You that is bigger than you, and a moving past the ego and into the soul. I invite you to immerse yourself in a participatory experience with nature. Instead of merely observing the world around you, you will be asked to plunge your whole being into creation through your five physical senses and your sixth sense, your intuition.

Notice if you have resistance to the idea of really letting yourself *be* in and with creation. What are the thoughts that come up around taking off your shoes, lying down on the earth, and surrendering your own agenda?

Find a place where you can experience a connection to creation, a nearby wooded area or park. If your weather is especially bad, you can do this in your imagination, but make a commitment to find a place on the earth itself after the thaw has arrived. Begin by walking around this space in the way you normally would with a contemplative posture.

Now take off your shoes and socks and stand barefoot on the ground. Allow some time to connect to the ground beneath you. Deepen your breathing; as you inhale imagine drawing up energy from the earth through your feet and up your legs. As you exhale, imagine sending down deep roots that will draw nourishment. Notice the temperature of the earth and the texture, whether it resists or yields. Walk a few steps and become fully present to the way the ground feels as you move across it.

Then kneel down and feel the earth in your fingers. Bring all of your senses to this experience, noticing texture, smell, sounds around you, any taste arising in your mouth, and what the earth looks like. Let yourself play for a little while. What might you have done as a child? How might your exploration have been more free and spontaneous? See if you can let that part of yourself have some time to explore.

Pause and notice how this experience is different from the contemplative walks you have been taking. Is there a qualitative difference? Notice this without judgment.

Look around you and explore the texture of tree barks, the feeling of plants between your fingers, and the smell of the earth. Open yourself to the sounds around you. Rather than reaching for sound, simply receive whatever it is you hear. When sounds arise, notice them and let them go. There is no straining in this exploration, just an opening to experience.

Then open yourself to the spirit and wisdom of this place. See if you might experience yourself connected to and woven together with this earth, these trees, and these flowers. Feel your relationship to the insects crawling under the ground or in the trees.

Open your heart as much as you can to receive other levels of awareness beyond your five senses. See if you can let go of trying to have a specific kind of experience, and simply sense yourself being here without agenda or goals. Notice what your experience is like now. What are you discovering in your own body?

Whether you are outside in intimate connection with the earth or exploring this in your heart's eye, let your exploration continue into a dance. What is it like to dance with the trees and the wind, the sun and the grass?

Response to the Meditation

To dance with the trees and the wind, the sun and the grass,
this morning feels like surrender, a deep warm surrendering, a release and relief that streams out towards eternity.

My mind isn't interfering, and neither is it afraid. It wants itself and the body to experience this side of bliss.

If I were a feather I'd be suspended in mid-air. The breeze would support me on all sides; I'd be adrift, weighed down by no thing yet a part of everything.

—Ivette Ebaen

Creative Exploration: "I Am" Poem

Say I Am You
I am dust particles in sunlight.
I am the round sun.

To the bits of dust I say, Stay.
To the sun, Keep moving.

I am morning mist,
And the breathing of evening.

I am wind in the top of a grove,
And surf on the cliff.

Mast, rudder, helmsman, and keel,
I am also the coral reef they flounder on.

I am a tree with a trained parrot in its
    branches.
Silence, thought, and voice.

The musical air coming through a flute,
A spark of a stone, a flickering

In metal. Both candle,
And the moth crazy around it.

Rose, and the nightingale
Lost in the fragrance.

I am all orders of being, the circling
    galaxy,
The evolutionary intelligence, the lift,

And the falling away. What is,
And what isn't. You who know

Jelaluddin, You the one
In all, say who

I am. Say I
Am You.

                    —Jelaluddin Rumi, *Rumi: The Big Red Book*

Read Rumi's poem above and then use it as a jumping-off point to write your own version of an "I am" poem. Let images arise spontaneously without editing, and continue returning to the words "I am" and listening for what parts of creation you long to identify with. When you remember yourself as an intimate part of nature, what images rise up?

Responses to the "I Am" Poem

I am . . . the sound of bird-song greeting
    the dawn
I am . . . the rustle of wind caressing the
    pines
I am . . . the glint of sunlight dappling the
    path through the woods
I am . . . the trickling creek—slow but
    steady toward the lake
I am . . . in the embrace of life, savoring
    the love of ancient friends

                    —Cynthia Helton

I AM the skates (a fish) jumping out of
the water as they gather dinner
I AM one with the Hibiscus,
Bougainvillea, palm tree, succulent
and grasses
I AM a container/pool where I can be
totally submerged and feel "baptized"
I AM morning fog, midday haze,
afternoon breeze and sunset.
I AM living fully in the moment

—Gracia Sears

I am midnight blue in starlit night;
I am early morning golden pink.
I am bare gray branches,
reaching out to touch the greens.
I am brown leaves crackling on the
ground.
I am the red topping on a woodpecker's
crest.
I am black rich soil,
shooting sprouts.
I am blossom, root, snoring mountain,
mist and snow.
Lake, brook, pond, river, bog, stone and
cliff
become
my arms, heart, knees, chest and feet.

I am they and they are me:
my body-earth;
my earth-body.

—Margo Nagle

Cool blades of grass
Caressing the soles of my feet
pebbles pushing against flesh
reminders of the daily ups and downs
fine puffs of breeze against my cheek
here it is then it's gone
changes ever so slight
crunching over the dry fall leaves
the firm soil around the remnants in the
    garden
Walking barefoot in November

—Pamela Phiefer Mathews

I am hope, fear, love and sadness. I am possibility. I am a
book being written.

—Bridget O'Grady

Movement Exploration

Yin Yoga: Sleeping Swan

Swan is the same pose as pigeon in more traditional yoga. I highly recommend visiting www.YinYoga.com for instructions on entering the
pose safely, especially if you have any knee issues. Essentially you come

to all fours and then bring one leg forward and bend it so that the bottom of your leg comes across your body on the floor. You can stay upright in full swan, or to deepen the stretch you can lean your upper body forward, letting your head be relaxed.

This is one of my favorite poses because it is a great hip opener. But I also love the experience of folding over my bent leg like a sleeping swan. I often ponder a poem by Rainer Maria Rilke called "The Swan" in which he describes the awkward lumbering of the swan on dry land and how, when it enters the water, it becomes graceful. Meditate while in this pose: What is your element? Where do you find the most ease? Nature has much wisdom to offer to us.

After completing one side, stretch out the leg that was bent behind you, perhaps coming up into downward dog if you are familiar with that pose and it is accessible to you. But any movement that feels good is perfect. Then be sure to come into the pose on the other side. Notice if your other leg and hip feel any different. It is completely normal if it does. Allow some time for rest following the pose on both sides.

Dance with Nature

This movement practice is an invitation to explore being in nature in an embodied way. You could begin with the earlier meditation in this chapter and really feel yourself as a part of creation around you. Allow the boundaries and resistance to shed away as much as possible.

Find a place where you can move your body gently in response to the nature around you. It might be your backyard, a local park on a quiet day, or another favorite place of respite. Notice what shimmers forth and draws your attention; then see if you might make shapes in your body that mirror what is calling to you. If a tree has a strong presence for you, embody the tree, extending your arms upward, perhaps swaying. Feel your feet planted firmly on the earth. If a bird is capturing your attention, spread your arms like wings and play with the experience of flying in your imagination.

Let your body reach, bend, lean, lie down, or whatever you feel inspired to do by the world around you. With each shape you take on, allow some time to breathe into it as if it were a yoga pose. Notice your experience as you embody this part of the landscape or creature. Crawl on the ground like a caterpillar. Bend in the breeze like the flowers.

When you have explored several different forms, come to a quiet resting pose for several minutes. Close with some time to journal what you noticed and discovered.

Reflection Questions

- What does the earth have to teach you about living in your body in a loving way?
- What do you notice for yourself about making regular connections with the earth? How does your body respond? Your thoughts? Your feelings?
- When you allow your body to connect to its wild nature, what longings do you discover?

Closing Blessing

Body Psalm for Gardenias

Return to the fragrance
of the interior palace
where a hundred gardenias
live inside your chest
You are not only breathing
but being breathed
by the aroma of sweetness
where petals of sorrow
t r a n s f o r m
to the sounds and smells of
s p a c i o u s n e s s
All along there is another listening
guiding you from within
decongest your hearing

and listen to the inner ear
where a deeper stillness
calls you back
to the garden
where you smell, touch and hear
the pulse of creation
beating within you
and you are named back
to your heartsong
and dare to live
in your own
e x t r a v a g a n c e.

—Celeste Snowber

Chapter 10

Coming Home to Your Body: The Vocation of the Body

If only we can bring the wisdom of the body to consciousness, spirit will no longer be homesick for home.

—Marion Woodman, *Leaving My Father's House*

If you listen to the wisdom of your body, love this flesh and bone, dedicate yourself to its mystery, you will one day find yourself smiling from your mirror.

—Jill Mellick, *Coming Home to Myself*

I believe deeply that caring for the body is central to my vocation and calling; the two are knit together so that I can't separate how I treat my body from how I respond to the ways God calls me into the world. I nurture sabbath rhythms in my life and resist as much as I can the hold a culture of doing can have on me. I replenish so I can have something to offer to others.

However, these last few years I have also been asking the question of how I might not just see caring for my body—the vehicle for my expression in the world—as woven together with how I care for my vocation. I am also beginning to see *the care of my body itself as my primary vocation* regardless of how that facilitates my *doing*. This is a subtle but profound shift I have been working to integrate in my life. What if beneath the many important things I am called to do in this world, the most fundamental of those is to cherish my body being, this sacred vessel that is my soul's address? I cherish my body not just so I can work harder but also because my body, just as it is, is the most profound voice of wisdom I can access and the very shape of my being in the world.

What if you are in this world to learn to cherish and adore this exact vessel that is your birthright? How might this change your relationship to your body?

I am convinced that learning to live in our bodies, to truly embrace both the profound dignity and pleasure as well as the tenderness and sometimes excruciating vulnerability of them, is the most important work we can do. Our vocation is to make sure the needs of bodies are cared for: that all bodies are well nourished and touched in loving ways, given shelter and the medicine they need, and not blown to bits with guns and bombs or forced to experience other violence or neglect. We need to address the more subtle ways we do violence to our bodies through overworking, pushing ourselves, and eating food sprayed with pesticides. When we love our own bodies, we start to feel invested in making sure the bodies of others, both human and animal, have love and care as well.

In this act of honoring bodies, we also honor the Greater Body. If we took bodies absolutely seriously, these very delicate containers of flesh and fluid, wouldn't we also begin to love the wider body more deeply of which we are a part, the communion of all people and creation, and that one Great Body that pulses and breathes with the presence of the Creator? Isn't that what the incarnation is all about?

Bodyfulness

> What if thought is not born within the human skull, but is a creativity proper to the body as a whole, arising spontaneously from the slippage between an organism and the folding terrain that it wanders? What if the curious curve of thought is engendered by the difficult eros and tension between our flesh and the flesh of the earth?
>
> —David Abram, *Becoming Animal*

I am intrigued by the fact that we have terms for mindfulness, which means to bring ourselves fully present to the moment. There is soulfulness, which speaks to a sense of deeper meaning of things. Thoughtfulness refers to our kindness and care. If we can be mindful, thoughtful, and soulful, what would it mean to be *bodyful*?

I think we need to start working toward a new language for our bodies and how we relate to them, how we see ourselves as woven intimately together with them, and the way they offer us the most profound kind of wisdom for life. For me, bodyfulness would mean a willing descent into the wilderness of my body, to stay and listen and explore, and to delight and dream in that dark space of unknowing where things don't move in straight lines according to plan. It would mean that each morning I would awaken and listen for how my body wanted to be nourished that day, through food, movement, and the pleasure of touch.

Bodyfulness would mean that I inhaled deeply and allowed my breath to find all the places within that need softening. I would lavish my senses with delights, knowing they were a portal to the divine presence. I would allow the waves of my emotions to travel through me, knowing they had holy purpose as well. I would dance each day as often as possible and rest deeply, knowing I was offering myself healing balm.

After working with these ideas for a while, I discovered that Christine Caldwell, a professor at Naropa University, had a similar thought and wrote an intriguing article called "Mindfulness and Bodyfulness: A New Paradigm" for the *Journal of Contemplative Inquiry*. She describes in the article how words such as *mindful, thoughtful, heartful,* and *soulful* all describe a particular positive quality of attentiveness. Why is *bodyful* missing from the conversation? I am reminded here of the image I shared at the beginning of this book of the body as the last unexplored wilderness. Perhaps we need new language to express the next frontiers of exploration.

Caldwell describes bodyfulness, saying, "Bodyfulness is at its heart a contemplative practice, and this distinguishes it from embodiment for this reason. Bodyfulness can be cultivated by conscious, disciplined activities that increase our capacity to first be embodied, then increasingly bodyful."[1] She goes on to describe our bodies as not things we have but an experience we are; bodies are subjects rather than objects, although we regularly objectify them. Bodyfulness also awakens us to our relationship with other bodies through empathy, attunement, and bonding.

Saying No to the Violence of Modern Life

> To allow oneself to be carried away by a multitude of conflicting concerns, to surrender to too many demands, to commit oneself to too many projects, to want to help everyone in everything, is to succumb to the violence of our times.
>
> —Thomas Merton

When I first read these words from Thomas Merton in a *Yoga Journal* article on the practice of *ahimsa*, or nonviolence, I was blown away. Suddenly I saw so clearly how all my doing, striving, and ignoring of my body, pushing her past her limits in service of some ego-driven need to be productive and competent, was participating in the very violence I claimed to reject in my life. It was a humbling and powerful moment to claim nonviolence on this deeper level of body and soul, to make a commitment to reject all the subtle ways I perpetuate violence against myself.

Robert Johnson is a Jungian analyst, and in his book *The Fisher King and the Handless Maiden* he writes,

> One faces the devil's bargains frequently when planning the structure of one's day. How much can one crowd into the day? How much can I get with minimum payment? How many times in the day does feeling take second place to practicality? How many days go by without music or a sunset walk? How many vacations are half-spoiled because the energy has been spent in a dozen devil's bargains before one even gets there.[2]

When we choose efficiency over love, we sever ourselves. When we decide to sacrifice our body's needs, we lose something essential. Later, Johnson goes on to describe the frightening experience we often have when we are in the space of nothing happening. He describes this nothingness as the opportunity to accumulate healing energy: "To have a store of energy accumulated is to have power in back of one. We live with our psychic energy in modern times much as we do with our money—mortgaged into the next decade. Most modern people are exhausted nearly all the time and never catch up to an equilibrium of energy, let alone have a store of energy behind them. With no energy in store, one cannot meet any new opportunity."[3]

Reading those words, I recognized how, even though I try to live as debt free financially as I can, I store up energetic debts that are impossible to catch up with unless I make the choice to consciously slow down, to let go of what is not needed. A question I love is this: What is of the essence? I find it to be really vital for my ongoing discernment.

I understand there are bills to pay and commitments to others. I struggle often with the need to support myself financially and giving myself enough rest, time, and space. And while it is not an easy balance, I also believe it is one of the most important decisions I make, this choice on behalf of my body, to live from a place of bodyfulness and honoring my primary vocation.

Ally on the Journey: Mary, Mother of God

> Mary said, "Here am I, the servant of the Lord; let it be with me according to your word." Then the angel departed from her.
>
> —Luke 1:38

We welcome in our final member to our circle of allies. So much of Mary's story is a story about bodies. In the Annunciation, the angel comes to ask for Mary's consent, her holy yes, to the divine indwelling of the Spirit in her physical body. The journey she embarks upon is contingent upon her flesh being willing.

After the conception of Jesus, Mary visits Elizabeth, and the two pregnant women share a beautiful moment of embodied knowing. It is said that the child Elizabeth was carrying "leaped in her womb" in recognition of Jesus' presence in Mary. This is a wonderful affirmation of the way our bodies can know and celebrate things our thinking minds may not be aware of yet.

Mary is also present at Jesus' crucifixion and death. Both birth mother and death mother, we see Mary standing at the foot of the Cross and tending to her son's body. Invite Mary to be present with you and to help you cherish the experiences of both birth and death in your own life. Ask her to help you remember the sacredness of your body. Know that she has felt your joy and suffering. Know that she blesses you with lavish and unconditional love. Rest into her embrace.

Practice: Obedience and Saying Yes

> I am a feather on the breath of God.
>
> —Hildegard of Bingen

Previously we have explored stability and conversion, two vows Benedictines would take. Now we arrive at the third. The root of the word *obedience* means "to hear." And while in monastic communities there was some sense that the monk would be obedient to the abbot or abbess, the deeper meaning of this vow was the commitment to listen to God's movements and to respond to those.

Hildegard of Bingen offers this beautiful image of being a feather on the breath of God. This is a radical act of yielding ourselves, surrendering our expectations about how our lives should go, and embracing things as they really are. Hildegard invites us to say yes to where God might carry us. What would it mean to offer obedience to the divine presence speaking through our bodies?

Obedience means the radical yes to God's daily invitations. It means making space to hear and see those shimmering moments. It means saying yes to what I discover there in the stillness. Holy pause and holy yes seem to dance together.

As you listen and respond to God's daily invitations, let this also be a time of exploring the vow of obedience as it is revealed in your body. What does it mean to listen deeply to your body's longings for movement and stillness, saying yes to them in whatever way is appropriate for you?

As we near the end of this journey together, I want to invite you to really listen in the coming days, even more than you have already. See if you might discover new places for insight and wisdom to come forth from tissue and tendons, muscles and bone. The materials and reflections from our program will offer food for a long time; there is much integration to take place. Trust that what you have done already is enough. Trust that your body already knows what it needs. Trust that your body can reveal to you the very path forward you are called to take as body guardian and protector, as body cherisher and lover.

My experience is that this act of trust in your body's wisdom builds on itself. Again and again I have made choices from this deeper wisdom and been rewarded in ways I couldn't have anticipated. Each time I trust and I discover that, yes, this is exactly what I needed, I am offered more courage for the next yes.

Meditation: Welcoming Yourself Home

I invite you into a final meditation experience to help you integrate the journey you have made. Begin by finding a comfortable space and deepen your breath to bring your awareness fully into your body. Allow yourself a few minutes to settle in and slow yourself down.

Begin by remembering the gift of viriditas, the greening power of God, and as you breathe in, inhale that greening life force. As you exhale, release whatever stands in the way of your own body's greening. Then drop your awareness back to your breath, that simple gift that sustains you moment by moment. Let yourself be filled with this life-giving breath, and savor the way it fills you. Then let that savoring extend outward to any sense experience you are having in this moment. What are the smells, sounds, tastes, images, and textures around you? Which ones might you savor and offer gratitude for?

As you continue to breathe, draw your awareness down to your heart, and notice what you are feeling right now without judgment or trying to change it. Sit with the experience while breathing gently and deeply. See if you might let the emotion simply move through you like a wave. Notice what your heart's desire is in this moment of time. As thoughts and judgments arise, simply notice them and let them move on. When criticism enters in, release your grasp and see if you might send it on its way.

Make room for whatever grief might need to visit, staying connected to your breath and knowing you can pause this meditation at any time if the experience becomes too intense. Honor the places of lament still living in you, and commit to make space to mourn as much as needed in the days and weeks to come.

Remember the profound gift of the incarnation, that truth that God is made flesh. Breathe in again and imagine God animating your body. See the Spirit molding you at the moment of your creation and exclaiming, "That's *good*!"

Allowing some more deep breaths, notice if there is a space on the other side of the lament and grief where joy might live. Let your breath connect you to everything that breathes, and open yourself to a connection and sense of communion beyond your own limited self.

Taking a few more deep breaths, expand your awareness to embrace the earth body. Feel yourself breathing along with all of the creatures and plants and trees. Rest into this awareness for a while. Connect to your own body as an animal body.

When you're done, whisper the words "Welcome home" to yourself, and let your breath gently carry you back to the room.

Creative Exploration: Write a Love Letter to Your Body

I invite you to make some space to curl up—perhaps in your sensual altar space with anointing oil, soft throw to wrap yourself in, and delights to savor—and make a love offering to your body in words. Imagine that you are being reunited with a long lost lover, someone who once knew you so intimately, someone you could trust implicitly. But there has been distance and wounding, and so this letter is a beginning, an attempt to make amends and make new commitments.

Don't think this through too much; just let the words unfold. Keep checking in with your body, and ask what words it wants to hear from you.

Responses to the Love Letter

Dear Body,

It's amazing for me to realize that you and I have been together for more than sixty-seven years now. Sometimes it's been a really difficult relationship. I'm sorry for all the pain and hard times you've gone through and for when I haven't understood you or taken care of you how you needed. I've sure tried, but it hasn't always worked out so well. We've had some wonderful times and been to some wonderful places together, though. I'm lucky to have you, all of you, including the parts that hurt. I'm so grateful because without you I wouldn't be me. I don't know how much more time together we still have, and some of it will probably be hard. But I promise to love you and appreciate you and do the best I can for us. Shall we dance?

—Cindy Read

Dear body, lovely body,

You are such a good gift, deeply, profoundly good. How faithfully you carry me! How resilient and strong you are! How fragile and tender! How beautifully and wonderfully made!

Forgive me, dear body, for how I have ignored you, pushed you, ridiculed and attacked you. How I have given you garbage when you were hungry for nourishment. How I made you work when you were longing for rest. How I treated you with violence when you asked for peace.

Dear body, sweet friend, I want to do better. I will do better to treat you with the dignity and care you deserve.

I will learn from you how to be in this world in ways that nourish and heal.

I will care for you, offering you gifts of rest and play so that love may blossom.

I will see you. I will gaze upon your beauty and rejoice!

I will listen to you—to your wisdom, your desires, and your needs.

Body of mine, how wonderful you are. Hands that create and touch with love, feet that run and dance, a soft belly tender and warm, strong limbs and fragile organs.

Thank you, dear body, for what a faithful friend you've been. I will love you better, dear friend. I will.

—Stephanie Warner Jenkins

Body Blessing

Deep peace to the running blood within you.
Deep peace to the flowing air within you.
Deep peace to the stretching muscles within you.
Deep peace to the quiet bones within you.
Deep peace to the shining skin around you.
Deep peace of the infinite peace to you.
Deep peace to you my friend.

—Elaine Breckenridge

Movement Exploration

Yin Yoga: Sphinx

You are invited to try one more yin yoga pose. As always, if this pose doesn't work for your body, try a different one that does. There is no need to fit yourself into how you think your body should be shaped.

Sphinx is essentially the yin version of cobra, which is a gentle back-bend. Come to the floor and lay face down. For some this might be enough of a backbend. If you would like to move a little deeper into the pose, slowly, gently, and with mindful awareness lift your upper body up from the floor and use your forearms to prop yourself up. Keep your head and back soft and relaxed.

Bring an intention to deeply honor your body in this time through reverence and attention. As with the previous poses, bring your breath to places of holding and tightness in your body, mind, and heart, softening as much as you can.

If the stretch becomes too intense, lie back down again for a few breaths. Always honor your body's limits. Let this be an opportunity to simply pay attention to your inner experience. As we come to the end of our journey together, hold the invitation to say yes to your body as you move through your practice. Notice where in your body you feel any response.

Dance of Celebration

This is the end of our journey together. Play some music and allow yourself a dance of celebration at the work you have done and the new intimacy you have created with your body. Let your body dance in any way she desires.

This is the time to listen into your body and see if there are places you have still been holding back and explore what it might be like to gently open those portals within. Honor that this is an ongoing journey: you don't have to have it all figured out; you get to continue the dance.

Reflection Questions

- What is the great yes that is blossoming forth within your body?
- Were there any surprises for you in writing a love letter to your body?
- What did you notice in paying attention to the rhythms and seasons of your breath?
- What have been the gifts and graces, as well as challenges and struggles, in this journey for you?

Closing Blessing

Body Psalm for Home

Know this is not your home
but you live in-between
the stars, moon and sea
where you resonate
near edges and borders
shore of rocks and waves
land and river
the space with those
you practice love
Home is not a house

condo, villa or studio
but how you dwell
in each place of your life
there are as many spaces
as there are vegetables
and plant species.
Take comfort in unrest
and know we are all made
for something more
between particles and stardust
the living One is within
your chest and breast
and lives in the ache
of your longing to belong.
The world is temporary
but the love you know and feel
for daffodils and dance
children and creativity
friends and fauna
music and manna
endure.
Love breaks form
as you were made from dust
You carry the universe
within you
the mark of great longing.
Don't be fooled
by quenching with false waters
Retire into the life
created from the inside out
an eternal home
a heaven within.
Know the earth
is inside and outside you
here is the space for taking care

of your precious essence.
Make peace with your desire
and be brave
to know you are enough
a home unto yourself.

—Celeste Snowber

Conclusion

This blessing takes
one look at you
and all it can say is
holy.

Holy hands.
Holy face.
Holy feet.
Holy everything
in between.

Holy even in pain.
Holy even when weary.
In brokenness, holy.
In shame, holy still.

Holy in delight.
Holy in distress.
Holy when being born.
Holy when we lay it down at the hour of
    our death.

So, friend,
open your eyes
(holy eyes).
For one moment
see what this blessing sees,
this blessing that knows
how you have been formed
and knit together
in wonder and
in love.

Welcome this blessing
that folds its hands
in prayer
when it meets you;
receive this blessing
that wants to kneel
in reverence
before you:
you who are
temple,
sanctuary,
home for God
in this world.

—Jan Richardson, "Blessing the Body"

We have traveled a long way through these ten chapters. The descent into the wilderness of the body is its own kind of pilgrimage. A pilgrimage is a journey taken with intention, where we willingly court holy disruption to upend our assumptions and expectations.

As we reach the end of this experience, my hope is that you have found yourself gently undone in all the best ways. I hope you have found a wide variety of tools and practices to support you in your continuation of this journey home, which you will be on for the rest of your life.

May you continue to show up for yourself and your experience in compassionate and open-hearted ways. May you continue the exquisite journey into the depths of your own wildness to find your way home.

Acknowledgments

This book has been incubating for many years and is the fruition of much of my own inner exploration as well as exploration through the companionship of some amazing women.

I want to thank my dear teaching partner, cocollaborator, and friend, Betsey Beckman. Betsey is a gifted liturgical dancer with a background in movement therapy. Working with her over the years has definitely been key in helping me to reclaim my own embodied wisdom and joy.

I am very grateful to Molly Lannon Kenny, the founder of Samarya Center Yoga in Seattle, Washington. The first time I looked at her studio website I wept because of the many inclusive images I saw there. I practiced there with many wonderful and welcoming teachers and eventually completed the two-hundred-hour yoga teacher training program, which deepened my love of the practice even further. At Samarya, yoga is so much more than physical poses, encompassing the mental, emotional, and spiritual dimensions as well.

A deep bow of gratitude goes to Jamie Marich, the founder of Dancing Mindfulness, who has become a treasured colleague and guide in this work. Jamie read early versions of this manuscript and provided essential advice on how to make the work even more accessible for those who have a history of trauma.

To all of the movement teachers I have experienced over the years in a variety of modalities and forms, and especially to Aisling Richmond, a dear friend where I live now in Galway, Ireland, whose knowledge about somatics has deeply enriched my own embodied understanding, I offer my deep thanks.

I am so thankful for the amazing women who showed up for both the live and online versions of this material. I have learned so much from their engagement, reflection, and willingness to be vulnerable.

Special thanks to artist Karen Newe for creating the great images in this book to help clarify the yoga poses as well as to Celeste Snowber for allowing me to include her beautiful "BodyPsalms" that bring each chapter to such a rich conclusion.

I am always deeply grateful to the amazing team of editors at Ave Maria Press, especially Bob Hamma who accepted the book for publication and Amber Elder who helped shepherd it through the editing process. This is my sixth book with them, and I so value their enthusiasm over my work and unflagging support.

And finally, as always, my heart sings with gratitude for my beloved husband, John, who has taught me so much about unconditional love and the delights of living in a body.

Notes

1. Viriditas: Claiming New Body Stories

1. Benedicta Ward, trans., "Poemen 80," in *The Sayings of the Desert Fathers* (Kalamazoo, MI: Cistercian Publications, 1975), 178.

2. Breath: The Gateway to the Body

1. Translation from commentary by St. Irenaeus, *Against Heresies*, chap. XII, 1, 2, ANF, vol. 1, pp. 537–38.

3. Senses: The Threshold and Sacrament of Experience

1. Carey Ellen Walsh, *Exquisite Desire: Religion, the Erotic, and the Song of Songs* (Minneapolis: Augsburg Fortress, 2000), 7.

2. See Luke 5:27–39, 7:36–50, 9:10–17, 10:38–42, 11:37–54, 14:1–24, 19:1–10, 22:7–23, 24:13–35, and 24:36–53.

3. David G. R. Keller, *Oasis of Wisdom* (Collegeville, MN: Liturgical Press, 2005), 139.

4. Ward, *Sayings of the Desert Fathers*, 224.

4. Feelings and Desire: The Ocean of Emotion

1. Richard Rohr, *In the Footsteps of Francis: Awakening to Creation*, audio CD (Albuquerque, NM: Center for Action and Contemplation, 2010).

2. Gregory Mayers, *Listen to the Desert: Secrets of Spiritual Maturity from the Desert Fathers and Mothers* (Liguori, MO: Liguori Publications, 1996), 40.

3. Ibid., 46–47.

4. Learn more at RonnaDetrick.com.

5. Thoughts: The Inner Witness

1. See James Martin, S.J., *Becoming Who You Are: Insights on the True Self from Thomas Merton and Other Saints* (Mahwah, NJ: Paulist Press, 2013).

2. Chelsea Wakefield, *Negotiating the Inner Peace Treaty: Becoming the Person You Were Born to Be* (Bloomington, IN: Balboa Press, 2012).

3. Mayers, *Listen to the Desert*, 51. Emphasis mine.

4. Ward, *Sayings of the Desert Fathers*, 230.

5. Phil Cousineau, *The Art of Pilgrimage: The Seeker's Guide to Making Travel Sacred* (Newburyport, MA: Conari Press, 1998), 24.

6. Rainer Maria Rilke, *Letters to a Young Poet* (New York: Norton, 1934), 27.

7. Quoted in Christine Valters Paintner and Betsey Beckman, *Awakening the Creative Spirit: Bringing the Arts to Spiritual Direction* (New York: Morehouse, 2010), 44.

6. Exile and Lament: The Vulnerability of the Body

1. Walter Brueggemann, *The Prophetic Imagination*, rev. ed. (Minneapolis: Augsburg Fortress, 2001), 11.

2. Ibid., 3.

3. John Philip Newell, *A New Harmony: The Spirit, the Earth, and the Human Soul* (San Francisco: Jossey-Bass, 2011), 103.

7. Holiness Made Flesh: The Incarnation of Embodied Life

1. Richard Rohr, "Creation As the Body of God," in *Spiritual Ecology: The Cry of the Earth* (Port Reyes, CA: Golden Sufi Center, 2013), 236, Kindle ed.

2. James Nelson, "Doing Body Theology," *Healing Religion's Harm*, accessed August 2, 2016, healingreligion.com/2490/html/nelsondo.htm.

3. Cheslyn Jones, Geoffrey Wainwright, and Edward Yarnold, eds., *The Study of Spirituality* (Oxford: Oxford University Press, 1986), 253.

4. See *Our Lady, Dominic, and Ignatius* by Betsey Beckman, Nina O'Connor, and J. Michael Sparough for more details about the nine ways of praying.

8. Ecstasy and Reclaiming Joy: Expanding Our Threshold of Tolerance

1. Robert A. Johnson, *Ecstasy: Understanding the Psychology of Joy* (San Francisco: HarperSanFransisco, 1989).

10. Coming Home to Your Body: The Vocation of the Body

1. Christine Caldwell, "Mindfulness and Bodyfulness: A New Paradigm," *Journal of Contemplative Inquiry* 1 (2014): 73.

2. Robert A. Johnson, *The Fisher King and the Handless Maiden: Understanding the Wounded Feeling Function In Masculine and Feminine Psychology* (New York: HarperCollins, 1993), 63–64.

3. Ibid., 93.

Additional Resources

Recommended Resources

Beckman, Betsey. *Dancing with Monks and Mystics*. DVD. 2015. Order online at AbbeyoftheArts.com.

Caldwell, Christine. *Getting Our Bodies Back: Recovery, Healing, and Transformation through Body-Centered Psychotherapy*. Boston: Shambhala, 1996.

Earle, Mary C. *Beginning Again: Benedictine Wisdom for Living with Illness*. Harrisburg, PA: Morehouse, 2004.

———. *Broken Body, Healing Spirit: Lectio Divina and Living with Illness*. Harrisburg, PA: Morehouse, 2003.

———. *Marvelously Made: Gratefulness and the Body*. Harrisburg, PA: Morehouse, 2012.

InterPlay. www.interplay.org.

Kolk, Bessel van der. *The Body Keeps the Score: Brain, Mind, and Body in the Healing of Trauma*. New York: Viking, 2014.

Marich, Jamie. *Dancing Mindfulness: A Creative Path to Healing and Transformation*. Woodstock, VT: SkyLight Paths, 2016.

Newell, J. Philip. *Echo of the Soul: The Sacredness of the Human Body*. Harrisburg, PA: Morehouse, 2000.

Owens, Tara M. *Embracing the Body: Finding God in Our Flesh and Bone*. Downers Grove, IL: InterVarsity Press, 2015.

Paintner, Christine Valters, and Betsey Beckman. *Awakening the Creative Spirit: Bringing the Arts to Spiritual Direction*. Harrisburg, PA: Morehouse, 2010.

Paulsell, Stephanie. *Honoring the Body: Meditations on a Christian Practice*. San Francisco: Jossey-Bass, 2002.

Ray, Reginald A. *Touching Enlightenment: Finding Realization in the Body*. Boulder, CO: Sounds True, 2008.

Ryan, Thomas, ed. *Reclaiming the Body in Christian Spirituality*. Mahwah, NJ: Paulist Press, 2004.

Taylor, Barbara Brown. "The Practice of Wearing Skin." In *An Altar in the World: A Geography of Faith*. San Francisco: HarperOne, 2009.

Winton-Henry, Cynthia. *Dance—The Sacred Art: The Joy of Movement as a Spiritual Practice*. Woodstock, VT: SkyLight Paths, 2009.

———. *What the Body Wants*. Kelowna, BC: Wood Lake Publishing, 2004.

Woodman, Marion, and Jill Mellick. *Coming Home to Myself: Reflections for Nurturing a Woman's Body and Soul*. Berkeley, CA: Conari Press, 1998.

Additional Online Resources for Trauma Recovery and Eating Disorders

Eating Disorder Recovery

National Eating Disorders Association. www.nationaleatingdisorders.org.

Mental Health and Addiction Recovery Resources

National Mental Health Clearing House. www.mhselfhelp.org.

Substance Abuse and Mental Health Services Administration: Treatment Locator. www.samhsa.gov.

Mental Health Recovery: Trauma Focus

Marich, Jamie. "Introduction to PTSD and Trauma, Abuse and Other Stress-Related Disorders." SEABHS: Southeastern Arizona Behavioral Health Services. Accessed August 23, 2016. www.seabhs.org.

———. Mindful Living Coping Skill Videos (Trauma-Informed). *Trauma Made Simple: Trauma and the 12 Steps*. Accessed August 23, 2016. www.traumamadesimple.com/videos.

Mental Health/Suicide Prevention: LGBTQ Focus

The Trevor Project. www.thetrevorproject.org.

Self-Injury Recovery

Recover Your Life. www.recoveryourlife.com.

Christine Valters Paintner is the online abbess for Abbey of the Arts, a virtual monastery offering classes and resources on contemplative practice and creative expression. She earned a doctorate in Christian spirituality from the Graduate Theological Union in Berkeley, California, and achieved professional status as a registered expressive arts consultant and educator from the International Expressive Arts Therapy Association.

Paintner is the author of nine books on monasticism and creativity, including *The Eyes of the Heart*; *Water, Wind, Earth, and Fire*; *The Artist's Rule*; *The Soul of a Pilgrim*; and *Illuminating the Way*. She is a columnist for the progressive Christian portal at Patheos. She leads pilgrimages in Ireland, Austria, and Germany and online retreats at her website, *Abbeyofthearts.com*, living out her commitment as a Benedictine Oblate in Galway, Ireland, with her husband, John.

AVE MARIA PRESS

Founded in 1865, Ave Maria Press, a ministry of the Congregation of Holy Cross, is a Catholic publishing company that serves the spiritual and formative needs of the Church and its schools, institutions, and ministers; Christian individuals and families; and others seeking spiritual nourishment.

———◦◉◦———

For a complete listing of titles from

Ave Maria Press

Sorin Books

Forest of Peace

Christian Classics

visit www.avemariapress.com

AVE MARIA PRESS
Notre Dame, IN
A Ministry of the United States Province of Holy Cross